Reclaiming Singleness

Maximizing Your Opportunities as a Young Single Man

Sam McManus

Singleness is not a curse. It is a gift—a privilege that should be stewarded for the glory of God. In this book, Sam shows how to do that. Sam shows us an ancient path, rooted in Scripture, pointing us to the most remarkable man who has ever lived: King Jesus. Who, by the way, was single. Enjoy the journey.
—**Dr. Chris Harper**, *Chief Storyteller and CEO, BetterMan*

As someone who is always trying to redeem my time for the glory of God and the good of others, I find *Reclaiming Singleness* to be a compelling guide that frames time as a divine gift, urging us to embrace every moment. The book challenges single men to invest in their spiritual growth and intentional living, while highlighting that singleness is not a problem to solve, but an opportunity to grow closer to God. *Reclaiming Singleness* offers practical advice and the potential for significant personal and spiritual returns. If you're a single man, this book is for you!
—**Jordan Raynor**, *bestselling author of Redeeming Your Time and The Sacredness of Secular Work*

Looking back at my life, I wish I would've taken my singleness a lot more seriously. I was never content with where I was and constantly found myself looking ahead. Sam has made a great resource for men, who like me need to take this time in your life more serious. It is so important to address these issues now so that you can be all God called you to be when the time is right to pursue a woman! Marriage is not the end all be all and I promise it won't fix all your problems. Let this book guide you through this season before you embark onto the next chapter!
—**Christian Huff**, *Founder, 4:8 Men*

Who you marry is arguably the most important decision you'll make this side of heaven. But what about the "who" for the woman you might marry? Who is that person becoming? And, if you never marry this side of heaven, but know Jesus, there will be a marriage supper one day and you'll be a guest of honor. Who is that person becoming? What I love about this book is that it's not just a book on singleness, it's a refreshing look at identity and who you're becoming. Written with humility and genuine compassion for young men, Sam provides an eternal perspective for living fully alive for the Kingdom of God in your season of singleness.
—**Joshua Straub**, Ph.D., *Co-founder and author, Famous at Home*

Reclaiming Singleness offers a powerful and timely exploration of what it means to be a single man through a biblical lens in today's culture. It challenges cultural stereotypes and provides a refreshing perspective on singleness, emphasizing purpose, identity, and spiritual growth. With practical wisdom and deep theological insight, this book empowers single men to embrace their unique season of life with confidence and clarity, grounding their journey in God's truth and preparing them for whatever He has in store. Who you are becoming today will prepare you for how God will use you tomorrow. Don't waste this valuable time of influence and preparation. I'm grateful for my friend Sam McManus, who has written such a helpful and timely book!
—**Jonathan Morrow**, *author of Welcome to College: A Christ Follower's Guide for the Journey and Cultural Engagement and Student Discipleship Director, Impact 360 Institute*

The grass isn't always greener on the other side. It's only green where you water it. God has you uniquely placed exactly where you are supposed to be. Learning to embrace that truth and maximize the season of life you're in is much easier said than done. *Reclaiming Singleness* is an incredible guide to help you learn to steward the season God has you in to the best of your ability.
—**Hampton Dortch**, *Host, Wake Up and Lead Podcast*

Reclaiming Singleness provides a comprehensive roadmap to fulfill the life God has for you and different ways you can take ownership of your life. This book shows that you have a high and noble calling right here and now in your singleness. Take back your God-given identify and do the work to become the man God has called you to be and watch Him transform you forever.
—**Matt Long**, *Host, No Man Is An Island Podcast*

Every person has a different story. Every story is filled with different chapters. Those chapters are seasons God uses to sanctify us. *Reclaiming Singleness* is an excellent resource for the single season of sanctification. Sam challenges and encourages men to steward the season they are in well.
—**Amanda Reed**, *Co-host, Living Out Loud with Alley & Amanda Podcast and Co-author, Living Out Loud's 30 Days of Encouragement with Alley & Amanda*

Reclaiming Singleness is more than just a guide—it's a call to arms for men in their singleness. Sam doesn't just offer advice; he equips you with the tools to turn this season into one of deep purpose and spiritual growth. His focus on identity and mission resonates deeply with the conversations I have on my podcast, where men are seeking to live fully for God, not waiting for some future moment to begin their journey. *Reclaiming Singleness* is a must-read for any man ready to embrace his singleness with intention and purpose today.
—**Carlton French**, *Host, The Single Man Podcast*

All rights reserved. This book is protected by copyright. No part of this book may be reproduced or transmitted in any form or by any means, including as photocopies or scanned-in or other electronic copies, or utilized by any information storage and retrieval system without written permission from the copyright owner.

Scripture quotations marked (NIV) are taken from the Holy Bible, New International Version®, NIV®. Copyright © 1973, 1978, 1984, 2011 by Biblica, Inc.™ Used by permission of Zondervan. All rights reserved worldwide. www.zondervan.comThe "NIV" and "New International Version" are trademarks registered in the United States Patent and Trademark Office by Biblica, Inc.™ Scripture quotations are from the ESV® Bible (The Holy Bible, English Standard Version®), © 2001 by Crossway, a publishing ministry of Good News Publishers. Used by permission. All rights reserved. The ESV text may not be quoted in any publication made available to the public by a Creative Commons license. The ESV may not be translated in whole or in part into any other language. Scriptures marked KJV are taken from the KING JAMES VERSION (KJV): KING JAMES VERSION, public domain. Scripture quotations marked (CEV) are from the Contemporary English Version Copyright © 1991, 1992, 1995 by American Bible Society. Used by Permission.

Copyright © 2025 by Sam McManus

ISBN 978-1-7364031-2-9

Library of Congress Control Number: 2024918040

Printed in the United States of America.

Cover Design by Austin King

Contents

Preface   *13*

Introduction: Singleness is Not the Problem   *17*

PART ONE
Uncover Identity

Chapter 1: Identity   *27*
Chapter 2: Identity Imperiled   *33*
Chapter 3: Identity Truth   *39*
Chapter 4: The Marks of Manhood   *47*
Chapter 5: Single for Life?   *57*

PART TWO
Find Freedom

Chapter 6: Let Freedom Ring   *67*
Chapter 7: Lust   *73*
Chapter 8: The Itch for Intimacy   *79*
Chapter 9: Irritating the Itch   *87*
Chapter 10: The Eight As   *95*
Chapter 11: Heart Over Habits   *107*
Chapter 12: How Habits Help   *113*

PART THREE
Notice Opportunities

Chapter 13: Establish Habitual Servanthood   *121*
Chapter 14: Cultivate Abiding in Christ   *127*
Chapter 15: Discover Financial Freedom   *137*
Chapter 16: Develop a Sound Body   *143*

Chapter 17: Labor Unconventionally   151
Chapter 18: Initiate Community   159
Chapter 19: Develop Leadership   167
Chapter 20: Export the Gospel   173
Chapter 21: Enjoy and Explore   179
Chapter 22: Pursue in Prayer   183

PART FOUR
Pursue Wisely

Chapter 23: What is This Whole Pursuing Thing?   191
Chapter 24: Pursuing Like Christ   195
Chapter 25: When to Pursue   199
Chapter 26: How and Where to Pursue   205

Acknowledgements   *215*

Preface

Like many singles, I lived for years in discontent. I knew I had problems—a lot of problems. And as I looked across the aisle, I saw those who were married living apparently content and blissful lives. I wanted marriage, and I wanted it badly. *If I could just get married*, I thought, *all my problems will just melt away!*

When I graduated college and escaped the busyness and social pressures of student life, I worked as a young professional in a large city, and I began to take ownership of my life. I went "all in" where God had placed me. I was still single, but I was learning that singleness affords so many opportunities that other seasons in life don't.

My new perspective allowed me to drill down into the depths of who I am as a man and a child of God. I began to turn to God's Word to help me understand my identity and my place in God's plan.

I also began to find new freedom in my life. The busyness of college had led me to sweep many of my sins under the rug. As I grew in my identity as a son of God and came to understand the privileges that awards, I peeled up the rug and addressed some of my most glaring issues.

Standing more confidently on my own two feet, I also began to completely maximize the season of life in which God had placed me. I got involved in my local church, wrote *The Prayerful Pursuit*, began graduate school, started a podcast, bought a house, discipled a handful of guys, and became a landlord. I was having too much fun as a single guy.

Yet, as I fully enjoyed the opportunities that my single life enabled, I noticed the Lord begin to put the desire for marriage on my heart again.

This was different than the desire for marriage I had experienced years before in college. No longer was I looking for a relationship to be like everyone else or to solve my problems and give me a happy life. Now I was looking for an opportunity to love and serve—both my future wife and the people who would be part of our life together. I prayed, and I prayed some more, and asked the Lord to lead me to the right woman if that was his will.

I went on many dates, but one girl kept popping into my mind. This girl would soon become my fiancé. Though she and I had both enjoyed our single years and what the Lord did in us individually through that season, she and I both knew the Lord was calling us to say goodbye to our single season and welcome the adventure of marriage.

In all of this, I was shocked, surprised, and grateful. For all my desire, I had never actually expected to get married. But, as I found through many conversations with friends, God often gives his children the gift of a spouse in seasons when they are deeply content as single people. It is sad to say goodbye to my single season, but I greatly anticipate my upcoming season of marriage.

I never planned to write a book about singleness, but I have felt the Lord prompt me to showcase what he has done during my single years in order to help other men do the same. The goal of this book is that you would have a new perspective on singleness, find contentment where the Lord has placed you, and be ready if it's his will to lead you somewhere new.

This book is broken up into four parts, each capturing an aspect of the experience of my single years. The first three parts of the book were written when I was indeed a single man. The last past, about what it looks like to pursue, was written just weeks before I proposed to my incredible fiancé.

This book outlines how God accomplished some incredible things through a guy who least expected it. By no means do I see marriage as the ultimate goal for me or for others, but instead I celebrate what God has done in my life and how he has taken a sinner like me and transformed me through the power of Jesus Christ. I haven't "arrived" in life, and I'm not sure I ever will, but I've seen the Lord do the incredible things and I am grateful for that.

This is a story about the journey of trusting God. It is worth celebrating that God chooses to use broken people to encourage, serve, and equip other broken people during this short life on earth.

I hope that this book will do just that.

Introduction

Singleness Is Not the Problem

The goal of life is not to get married. Your purpose in life is to worship God with what he has entrusted to you while living in submission to his will. If this means getting married, then great! But if this means staying single, then that's great too. Your goal should be to get to a place in life where you are more concerned about the will of God and maximizing what he has already given you, rather than trying to make him conform to your desires and wishes.

But let's face it; being a single guy can be tough. It can feel like every time you open social media, someone else is engaged, married, having kids, and you're just sitting on the couch trying to figure out what to have for dinner.

With so many of your friends continually getting married and with few resources available for single guys, it may leave you feeling like you have done something wrong. You can't help but wonder, *Will I be single forever?* or *What am I doing wrong that is leaving me single? When should I try to move from being single to pursuing a relationship? Is being single a bad thing?* If you're like me, you've wrestled with these questions as you've remained a single man.

Here's the deal: you are single now for a reason. You being single gives you opportunities that no other season in life can afford! You have the opportunity to learn more about who you are, grow in an area of life you need to grow in, and cultivate Christ-likeness.

Again, let me stress that the goal is not marriage. Marriage is an incredible gift from the Lord. Most Christian men who seriously consider whether God is calling them to singleness will find that He is not. But abandoning many of the other things the Bible commands us to in order that we can just find a spouse is not a wise strategy. The goal of your life should be aligning to God's will and seeking to honor him with your time, talents, and treasures.

Your singleness is not the problem you think it is. Instead, singleness just surfaces some of the biggest issues, lies, and struggles in your life and it highlights where you need to grow. Most people just blame singleness for all their problems, but in reality singleness is providing them an opportunity to address them and grow as a person.

Throughout the many years I have been single, my perspective on singleness has changed. For most of my single years, I experienced shame about my relationship status, and I would work hard to keep myself busy so that I would forget about the "failure" of still being single.

However, in the last couple of years, the Lord has slowed me down and allowed me to take some inventory of my life. As I have removed things from my calendar and built margin into my schedule, I have been able to pinpoint many of the issues that I need to work on in my life, and the Lord has been kind to give me time and space to do so. I want to encourage you to slow down in your singleness to allow the Lord to speak to you and to reveal things to you. It has been in my slower seasons of life where I have felt the Lord stretch, grow, and challenge me more.

Before we jump into how you can best spend your single years, we need to understand a few crucial truths about singleness first.

The Grass Isn't Greener Over There

Have you ever thought about how great it would be to get past being single? To be married would be just so blissful and it seems like so many of your problems would go away. Or maybe you've recently thought about other areas of your that you're frustrated in and considered, *Man, if I was just in better shape, I would be so content.* Or, *If I had just had a few more thousand dollars in my savings account, I would feel so secure.*

This is a hard part of life. You see, as humans, we never actually get to a point where we are content with everything. There is always more money, higher social status, deeper education, or more opportunities that we crave. Scripture affirms this in Ecclesiastes 1:8, where the writer says, "The eye never has enough of seeing, nor the ear its fill of hearing." As humans living on a sinful, fallen planet, we are always going have the natural desire for more and will be tempted to believe the lie that "if I just had this one thing, then I'd be content."

When it comes to singleness, for many guys the greener side is marriage. But let me break it to you: marriage is filled with challenges, obstacles, and struggles, just as singleness is! Though marriage can prove to be incredible and beneficial in its own ways, the Lord can work through singleness if we trust him to, and he will teach us great things.

So, if the grass isn't greener on the other side, we need to learn to honor the side of life that God has placed us on and the stewardship he has given us. That is there we will find contentment.

Marriage Won't Fix It

For years, I craved getting married because I was certain that all my problems would just go away. If I could just find the girl of my dreams, then I would stop looking at porn, stop lusting, and stop feeling lonely. I was ready to ride off into the sunset with my dream girl and just live happily ever after.

Unfortunately, forces in our culture from Disney down to our friend groups, and even our churches, conspire to convince us that marriage is the ultimate goal and that once you find your spouse, the troubles of life will seemingly melt away. But in many conversations with close married friends, many men have voiced that they wish they had spent more time during singleness working on some of things that they struggled with.

Your porn addiction, lying problem, lust habits, and money obsessions will not just dissolve once you say, "I do." You see, the truth is, marriage magnifies your problems. A friend once told me that marriage is like moving into a small apartment—you realize just how much baggage you actually have! Marriage will bring your pride, poor motives, and hidden sins to the surface. Marriage will also create new problems, and if you aren't used to addressing the current issues in your life, then it will be very challenging to do so in marriage.

Marriage will not fix your issues; it will surface them and add to them. That why it's important to invest in your single years to peel back the layers and grow yourself as a man right now.

Stop Trying to Be Perfect

Many single guys opt to remain single because they are aware of how many issues they truly have. While it is true that every human being on the planet has his or her own list of problems, it is important to realize that one will never be perfect on this side of heaven. In this book, I will be laying out actionable items that you can do as a single guy, but I don't want you to think that these items are me dangling a carrot in front of your face making you think that one day in this life you will be perfect and that you must achieve this perfection in order to date.

Instead, it's wise as a single guy to be intentional about where has placed you right now. As we will discuss later in this book, you shouldn't choose to be single forever just because you're not perfect yet, and there is wisdom in knowing when it is appropriate for you to date despite the issues and struggles you continue to face.

Here's what this book is not. This is not a guide to getting you on the shortest path to marriage. No. Instead, this book is designed to help you go all-in to the season of your life as a single guy right now. This is a journey of you beginning to steward everything God has given you well, even the smallest of things, so if you're looking for a ten-step guide to finding the woman of your dreams, then you might need to grab a different book.

This book is broken into what I call the four pillars of singleness. It is through these pillars that I have tried to extract the principles and commands from God's Word and communicate them for the single man.

First, we will focus on uncovering identity. Your success as a single—or married—person is going to depend on how you see yourself fitting into the grand scheme of things. When you understand that you belong to God and were made to worship and enjoy him, you will flourish. This will require you to seriously consider where you look for affirmation, and it will require a determined effort to lay aside your idols.

Next, we will focus on finding freedom. Once you understand who you are and who God is, you will be able to address some of the sins, struggles, and issues that are plaguing your life. These things are like dirt and grime that have collected on the windshield of your life, making it hard—if not impossible—to see where you're going and drive safely. You'll need to clean the windshield before you can move forward confidently.

Third, we will notice opportunities. As you are confident in your identity and work to free yourself of sin, it will be possible to go all-in on the opportunities that singleness affords you. I'll lay out ten unique opportunities that you will find in singleness.

And lastly, we will learn what it means to pursue wisely. As you consider pursuing a woman one day, we'll unpack what pursuit means, why men pursue, and how and where you can do it.

These are the pillars that I want to challenge you to adopt today so that you can begin to reframe your singleness. This is a journey, and it will take some work. But trust me, and follow these steps, and you'll have a roadmap for honoring God with your single years.

This book is not meant to be cozy. It will not require minimal action on your part with the promise that your life will completely change. Instead, this book will require work—intentional work. It will require embracing activity and rejecting passivity, stepping into habits, thoughts, and patterns that you have never tried before. It will require you to radically rewire some of the ways your brain has thought about certain things for years and to say no to your strong fleshly desires and yes to higher calling.

At the end of each chapter, I will ask a question for personal reflection. I will also some practical ways to put the chapter's content into action. I call these "single shifts." They are "single shifts" because they aim to change the way that you have been approaching singleness. They are "single shifts," too, because with each of these actions comes an opportunity to see how that one small change can impact your life and your future. Along with these, I suggest a prayer that will allow you to bring your experience with that chapter's topic to God. Many of these are prayers that I myself prayed as a single man.

It's time to shift to a new perspective of singleness with the hope of becoming a stronger, more content, man of God. I believe that as you seek to intentionally change one small single thing after the other, you will create massive change and major momentum in your life. These single shifts can over time completely change your life and have the power to make you into the man of God.

As God chose to create you, he made you so that you can bring maximum glory to his name. As we look at singleness, we realize that singleness presents an unbelievable opportunity to honor God and worship him. You don't need a spouse before you can bring God honor and worship. This time in your life, if stewarded well, can have massive return on investment not only in this life, but for eternity. As you use singleness to go beyond yourself and influence and serve others, you have the potential to radically change people's lives for eternity.

You have been entrusted with the season of life you have right now. Are you being a good manager of it? Are you willing and ready to step out in faith that God might have something incredible in store for you in this season of singleness that you find yourself in? Do you believe that you can truly be content and joy filled as a single man?

It's time to take a risk and step forward into potentially actually enjoying your single life.

Are you ready?

A Question
What problems have you expected to be solved once you get married?

A Single Shift
Spend some time journaling about what your life could be like if you found deep contentment as a single man. What would change if you were able to address and tackle some of your greatest struggles?

A Prayer
Lord, thank you for other men who have had the same struggles with singleness that I have. I pray now as I begin this book that you would speak

to me, convict me, and grow me as a man of God. Please use my season of singleness and the content in this book to make me look more like Christ. Amen.

PART ONE
Uncover Identity

Chapter One

Identity

Understanding your identity is one of the most important things to be doing right now, while you are single.

Identity is who you are. Your sense of identity is who you understand yourself to be. Your sense of identity informs your self-worth and influences your personal values. It determines your responsibilities, shapes your decisions, molds your thoughts, and fuels your sense of purpose. Your sense of identity is vastly important because who you understand yourself to be determines what you will choose to do.

Your identity impacts many areas of your life, including:
- What or whom you worship
- People you hang out with
- Your responsibilities
- The type of spouse you may pursue
- How you engage with others
- How you manage your time
- How you spend your money

The truth is that who you are today and how you act reveals what you believe about your identity. In fact, if you show me your schedule, your budget, and your relationships, I can tell you what your identity is rooted in.

Typically, in our culture today, people find their sense of identity in what they do. Ask most men in their fifties who they are, and they will likely tell you about their career. This is why many men have an identity crisis when they retire: because their identity is so wrapped around their jobs. Many men who have their identity wrapped up in material goods or even family can face identity crises later in life when they lose assets or when their kids move off to college.

For most people the "do" determines the "who," but as Christians we must be sure to order our lives in a way that allows the "who" to inform the "do." Since our occupations, obligations, and commitments change from season to season, it isn't wise or practical to attempt to identify ourselves by things that change. Our identity should be rooted first of all in our relationship with the unchanging God. When you know at the core of yourself who you are and whom you belong to, your actions will naturally align to this new identity.

Where you place your identity affects more than just yourself. I have seen too many guys enter marriage while finding their identity in the wrong places. This is bad for the husband, the wife, and the kids. It can cause blow ups of anger, thoughts of jealousy, and temptations to infidelity. It can instill fear in a wife and kids. Indeed, so many of the pains, divorces, and traumas that families go through could be eliminated if the husband was confident of his God-given identity. The truth is, your family tree can drastically change as you uncover and live from your God-given identity.

Identity also has a big correlation with pride and humility. In college, I knew I had a pride problem, and for years I would try to just "be humble," or at least appear humble. I'd do things like pretend I was listening to someone talk or offer to help someone in need even though I really didn't want to help. But humility is not something you can just choose to do. Instead, humility is a byproduct of your identity being rooted in the right place. In fact, most of the things you want in life, like belonging, acceptance, security, confidence, purpose, and love from others, are only fully achieved when your identity is properly sourced.

The truth is the problems we see on the surface often aren't true problems. They are symptoms. And that's what I think could be happening in your life right now. Your anger toward your current season, your complaining about life's circumstances, your working extra hard to achieve value are all not actually the true issues. These things, among others, are all signals that your identity is not in the right place. Indeed, much of the discontentment you feel in singleness is a sign of a deeper issue, an identity-issue that needs to be addressed.

Paul knew this. When Paul was writing letters to some of the very first Christians on earth, he saw identity as important concept to understand. In his strategy to teach others how to order their lives to look more like Christ's, Paul spent the first half of many of his letters telling the people how to source their identity in the right place before focusing on how they should live. Imagine if I wrote a book to encourage you with practical habits and disciplines, but instead of talking about what to *do* first, I spent more than half the time on who you are! (Actually, that is exactly what I'm trying to do here.) We must spend time understanding, reflecting on, and celebrating our identity before anything else. As we do so, so many of our other problems will take care of themselves.

We should recognize that God is ultimately the establisher of our identity. It is not you, your future wife, your parents, or anyone else. Instead, your identity has been determined by God before you were born.

In the coming chapters we will unpack what Scripture has to say about who you are and how to apply it in your life. The truth is, you have a new identity. Through Jesus's death and resurrection, you have access to a new personhood that grants you freedom and new life. The old has passed away, and the new has come (2 Cor. 5:17). The question is: Are you living from it?

This is one of the best things you can be working on while you are single, because so many men get this wrong. You must seek to take the time in your single season to uncover who you are. Don't let the world dictate who you are, or your work, or your wife; you must let your Creator tell you who you are.

A Question
If you had to use Scripture to define your identity, which passages would you use?

A Single Shift
Reflect on the various things you have found your identity in in the past. List out the phrases or statements that currently define and highlight your identity and consider how these identities might be affecting your life.

A Prayer
Lord, I thank you that you love me enough to give me a new identity and that you don't leave me to figure it out on my own. Show me where I am currently placing my identity and how it is informing my actions. Teach me to find my value in you alone and not in my own actions or social status. Thank you, Lord. Amen.

Chapter 2

Identity Imperiled

Before we jump into what your identity is through Christ, we must talk about the giant battle that is taking place against your identity. Here's the thing: this battle has always been happening. Attacks on identity are not new. Christians through the ages have had to learn how to sift through "the flaming arrows of the evil one" (Eph. 6:16, NIV) in order to reinforce and protect their true identities.

This might encourage you: Did you know that Jesus's own identity was also attacked? Yup, the man who lived a life without sin was still tempted to misplace his identity in something other than the truth.

We read about this in Matthew 4, when Jesus was led away into the desert for forty days and nights. While Jesus was there, Satan came to him and said, "If you are the Son of God, tell these stones to become bread" (v. 3, NIV). The attacks of Satan were targeting the very identity of Jesus. "If you are…" Satan said. The enemy was attempting to get Jesus to do something based on his identity. Satan was attempting to steal the identity of Jesus in order to build Satan's own kingdom and platform rather than God's.

We face the same attacks from Satan in our lives too. Maybe you've already experienced some today. Satan works hard to tempt you in the most opportune times to make you believe something vastly untrue about your identity, and he then tempt you to prove that false identity through action. Because identity is so important, it makes sense that this would be *the* thing that Satan would go after. It's like taking out the Pentagon if you want to attack the US military. Attacking your identity has the potential to shut down you down completely.

For years, Satan convinced me that my value and worth came through how my body looked. This led me to obsess over myself in the mirror, do insane amounts of cardio, and stress out when I couldn't see my abs. I believed that if I didn't measure up to the standards that I had set for myself when it came to my physical body, God and others wouldn't love me at all. This was a lie from Satan.

Satan is your biggest enemy, and he will sneakily attempt to make you believe something different about yourself that isn't true. And since your actions are attached to your identity, Satan has a better chance of getting you to *do* something bad if he can convince you that you *are* something bad first.

Since these attacks are happening so frequently, protecting your identity is going to be crucial. Because we aren't immune to the attacks that are to come (again, *Jesus's* identity was attacked!), we have to learn what to do when our identity is threatened.

This is also why failure can hurt so badly in our lives. When we fail at something that we place our identity in, it hurts badly.

Before we jump into the truths of who you are through Christ, I want to spend a few minutes getting you thinking about where you might be currently sourcing your identity. I am always shocked at how I can misplace my identity in the most random, unthinkable things. The truth is, there are hundreds of places you can accidentally put your identity, but these are five common ones where single men tend to find their identity:

Apparel

During my senior year of college, a mentor told me I was putting my value in the clothes that I wore. I tried to dress in the "country fraternity" style so that I would fit in with other guys on campus. Does wearing a certain brand make you feel more important? Or does dressing like a particular group of people give you more leverage in your friendships? If so, you might be putting your identity in your clothing.

Age

I am constantly shocked at how many men feel increasingly useless as they become older. On the contrary, it's unsettling how many young men feel unqualified to lead just because of their age. Have you delayed getting started on something because you're not at the right age? Maybe you feel unwanted because of how old you are. The reality is your age changes once per year, and putting your identity in something that is constantly changing is always going to be exhausting!

Associations

It is very easy to tie our worth and value into man-made groups, clubs, and organizations. If my team does well, I do well too. If my political party wins, then I'll be a better person. Maybe you've limited yourself because of the school you received your degree from. I think every man has made the mistake of finding purpose, value, and worth in some sort of group he has associated with. Being part of group is a wonderful thing with undoubtedly many benefits, but it becomes dangerous when it dictates your value.

Appearance

You're not the only guy who watches himself flex in the mirror. In fact, so many guys struggle with finding their value and worth in how they look, but almost no one talks about it. This can even be paralyzing to the guys who are (or think they are) overweight and obsess over their macros and how their mid-section looks in the mirror. Your identity cannot be wrapped up in what your body looks like. We are called to honor our body and to steward it well, but we can't put all our stock in our bodies. The bodies we possess came from dust and will one day return to dust after they serve us during our short time here on earth.

Assets

When you're a kid, having everything seems to be everything. So many adults still struggle with this today. People who own very little feel inadequate to make a difference or move forward in their life until they have what everyone else has. Assets can be a powerful tool to bless others and to reward ourselves, but it should never be where we find value. Do you feel less capable because of the type of car you drive, house you live in, or amount of money you have in your bank account? Does the size tire you have on your truck correlate with the dignity you feel? If an asset defines who you are, what is left to define you when the asset is gone?

These five things are by no means an exhaustive list of all the places where you could find your identity. In fact, these are just ones that start with the letter "A." There are hundreds of places you could extract your own value and worth from. These are just a handful of the ones where I have unintentionally found my value over the last few years, and maybe you have as well.

The enemy will constantly be trying to tempt you to place your identity in something worldly. When one temptation doesn't work, he'll be hiding around the corner with another temptation.

Only a life of gratitude to and worship of God can defend against the flaming arrow attacks from the enemy on your identity. Reinforcing what God says is true and good about you according to God can extinguish the violent attacks you experience.

God wants to take you from where you are now to somewhere greater. God doesn't leave people where they are. He sees the single guys who are stuck in the wrong identity and is gracious enough to help them become unstuck. You are not forgotten about! God is kind enough to grant *you* a new identity and a new purpose. You must begin to see yourself as God sees you. The journey is not promised to be easy nor quick, but you can embark trusting that God knows what he is doing.

So, now you know where you might be finding your identity. But where does God *want* you to find it? To that we now turn.

A Question

Among the five examples in this chapter, which misplaced source of identity tempts you the most? Are you tempted by something not on this list?

A Single Shift

Ask someone you trust, who knows you well, where they think you find your sense of value. Be prepared for a difficult conversation, and guard yourself from anger and defensiveness! Taking their advice and your own reflections, consider a fast you might take in the coming weeks that might help you reset your vision to God. (For example, if you find your identity in appearance, you might fast from designer clothes or hair products.)

A Prayer

God, I recognize that I am a sinful person and that I am prey to the enemy's attacks. Forgive me for finding my value, worth, and identity in things of this world. Convict me of placing my worth in things I'm not even aware of, and speak through my community to reveal these patterns to me. Help me to be like your Son, Jesus, who knew who he was and operated confidently from his identity. Amen.

Chapter 3

Identity Truth

Hopefully you are beginning to see how easy it is to put your identity in something of this world. Hopefully you are beginning to pinpoint a handful of the unhealthy places where you source your identity.

I'll say it again: realizing and working on this is one of the greatest things you can be doing while you are a single guy. Remember: where your identity lies is where you will derive your sense of worth and value. Identity also informs your responsibilities, shapes your decisions, molds your thoughts, and fuels your purpose. Identity is important!

If we know that what we believe about ourselves will inform the way that we act, then it is critical that we view ourselves in light of truth. The good news is that you and I have been given a new identity from which to live. The fascinating thing is that this new identity does not come from something that you or I did. And though we might have to remind ourselves of this new identity daily, it is not something that we have to earn anew each day. No, you have been *given* a new identity through your faith in Jesus Christ, and it is a gift that God does not take back.

As you seek to live out our single years in a way that honors God, understanding your identity is crucial. In fact, it is understanding your identity in Christ that will make everything else in this book possible.

There are many truths that capture who you are as an adopted child of God. Let me give you four that I think will help you.

Son of God

When an orphaned child is adopted into a family, he or she takes on a brand-new identity. Furthermore, when parents decide to adopt, they do so understanding that the child they want has likely had a very challenging life up to that point. They will joyfully and gladly welcome them in even though the child is not perfect and may come with many challenges. In the same way, God the Father has chosen to adopt you as a son despite your sins, which he is well aware of. Paul tells us in Galatians, "You are no longer a slave, but God's child" (4:7 NIV). This adoption as a son did not come from because of something you did; rather, it is the gift of God (see Eph. 2:8). God, knowing that you are a sinner, has chosen you to be part of his family as a son.

When an orphan is adopted, he or she will be considered a child of his new parents with full rights and privileges alongside their biological children. They are to be protected, sustained, cared for, and loved by the new parents. He or she might even be left an inheritance when the parents pass away. In the same way, God grants you the full rights and privileges that come with being his son. The Lord has promised to protect you, sustain you, and provide for your needs. God also makes his children heirs in the kingdom of God in the life to come. As it says in Galatians, "Since you are his child, God has made you also an heir" (4:7 NIV). There are so many privileges that come with being adopted into God's family!

Through faith in God's Son, Jesus, you have become adopted into the family of God. Your new identity is birthed. You become a child, a son in the family of God with other sons and daughters who are chosen as God's people. Paul writes it this way in Ephesians: "For he chose us in him before the creation of the world to be holy and blameless in his sight. In love he predestined us for adoption to sonship through Jesus Christ, in accordance with his pleasure and will" (1:4-5).

God has adopted you as a son, and living from this identity as his child will completely transform your life. Finding your value and your worth through what God says about you will change the way you act day-to-day. Knowing that you have been adopted into God's family, despite your sin, should lead you to be enamored with what God has done and live a life of gratitude and devotion unto the Lord!

Image of God

Scripture tells us that Adam and Eve were created in the image of God (Gen. 1:26). To be "made in the image of God" has some powerful implications for your identity today.

The Greek translation of the word *image* can also be rendered in English as the word *icon*. An icon is something small that represents a greater or bigger being that might not be seen at the moment. For example, the logo on your shirt that represents a company that designed it is a kind of icon. With this in mind, you can begin to think of yourself as a little icon roaming around Earth reflecting the very image of God. Indeed, you are made in the image of God!

You yourself are a small representation of the presence of God here on earth and you will begin to understand more accurately who you are in this world as you live from this. God created Adam as a smaller representation of himself who would point back to the vastness and indescribability of a bigger and greater God.

Adam and Eve marred the image of God when they sinned. Sin blemished and flawed the perfect image of the King that God has instilled on his people. The great news is that this image is now restored in Christ, and we are now reflecting God's image fully as we abide in Christ.

God has chosen you as an "icon" and has adopted you into his lineage that has been continuing since Adam. Your uniqueness points back to the uniqueness of a big God. What an incredible identity truth to live from!

Temple of the Holy Spirit

As the Israelite people moved throughout the nation of Israel, God established a portable tabernacle as his place to dwell among his people. After years of dwelling in the tabernacle, God employed Solomon to establish a more permanent place to dwell. Through Solomon's intentional and marvelous work, a large, new temple was built in the city of Jerusalem and this is where people would go to encounter the Lord. For centuries, God made his presence known and remained close to his chosen people through the tabernacle and the temple, but later Christ would change that.

After Christ's death and resurrection, God re-established his dwelling place among his people. No longer would God dwell in a man-made structure in Israel, instead God now would dwell through his spirit living inside his chosen people today.

Scripture says that God has chosen you to be a temple too. Paul says to you and me that our "bodies are temples of the Holy Spirit, who is in you, whom you have received from God" (1 Cor. 6:19 NIV). This means that when you become a Christ follower, you are given the gift of the Holy Spirit living inside of you. Before Christ, God dwelt among his people but his chosen nation was unable to access his very presence. But now, through Christ, you have been given the Holy Spirit to live inside you, and you have become a temple-tabernacle that houses the very presence of God!

Jesus's death and resurrection made this possible, and he joins you and I together with other temples to create a dwelling in which God lives by his Spirit—that is, the church (Eph. 2:21-22). God's way of being present has shifted from a physical building to us as followers of Jesus Christ. We now operate as mini sanctuaries of worship throughout the world (1 Cor. 6:19). You can take on the identity of temple of God suitable for his purposes here on earth.

Disciple Maker

God commissioned Adam and Eve to glorify him by creating more image bearers. God has commissioned us to glorify him by multiplying disciples. This is how Jesus glorified God, and we can too. We are to "go and make disciples" (Matt. 28:19 NIV). As a temple of God's presence, you are called to steward your body-temple as an instrument to create more disciples here on earth.

Luke records what Jesus said about being a disciple of Christ: following Christ will mean denying yourself (14:27), being willing to give up everything (14:33), and looking different than the rest of the world (14:34). Just as Christ displayed obedience to his heavenly Father, so you too must display obedience to God's commands as his disciple.

As one reflects on our undeserved adoption as sons and the many blessings and gifts that come as being a child of God, one should be overwhelmed with gratitude and humility toward Christ. This gratitude and thankfulness to God should serve as a foundational motive to you as you go out unto the world and tell others about him.

Since our entire identity operates with the purpose to bring God the glory and honor that he deserves and desires, we must remind ourselves that any identity contrary to sonship in God is in direct conflict with operating and living how God intends his people to live. When you and I find our identity in things like clothes, who we associate with, or our status, we shift from choosing to worship God wholeheartedly to worshipping ourselves, other people, or the world instead. And because identity shapes action, the identity that we take on informs our action on earth.

The identity of being a son and part of God's eternal family is a blessing, not a burden, because you were chosen by God to bear his presence and witness and have been spared from eternal damnation. We cannot create our identity. Rather, it is given to us by the Creator, who has and always will be in full command and control of how he receives worship and praise.

It's important to remember that the point of living in the new identity is not to make your life easier. It is to give God the worship he enjoys and to make yourself more effective and available in full surrender for the kingdom of God so that you can create more people who enjoy worshipping God.

The beautiful thing here is that unlike how your identity rooted in worldly things has the ability to change, these truths cannot be changed or stolen. The book of 2 Corinthians tells us that Christ has "set his seal of ownership on us" (2 Cor. 1:22 NIV). Christ's identity for you is essentially branded, tattooed, or stamped on to you. It will not change; you are a chosen son of God set a part for good works. How comforting is this!

Your contentment in singleness will be accelerated and sustained through uncovering your identity in God. The degree of your contentment in singleness is directly related to your understanding and belief in your identity from God. Remind yourself of who you are in Christ. What a gift it is to be called a son of God!

Since our actions align to what we believe about ourselves, when we operate from an identity in Christ we can hope for a renewed mind and an overcoming of the flesh to better order our lives around how God has created and called us. Your identity has already been spoken. Now it is time to operate from it!

A Question
How does knowing that God chose me to be his son change my perspective on how I should act as his child?

A Single Shift
Find verses about your identity and start committing these to memory. In my Bible, I have identity-related verse marked with blue sticky notes. Write out these verses and put them somewhere, like your bathroom mirror, where you will see them daily.

A Prayer
Dear God, thank you for choosing me as your son. Though I live in the twenty-first century, I recognize that you have been working through humanity for millennia. Thank you that even though man sinned against you, you still chose to dwell among your people. Thank you that through the death of your son and his resurrection, we now have access to you anywhere we are. Thank you for living inside of me and allowing me to be a place of your presence. Amen.

Chapter 4

The Marks of Manhood

Every guy at some point wonders if they are actually living up to being a man. I would imagine you, as a single guy, have wondered the same thing. As we've discussed in previous chapters, the biggest attack you and I will face is on our identity. Satan loves to attack your manhood and make you feel insecure about doing manhood "right."

As you uncover what your identity is, it is important to also uncover what is true about you and the calling that comes with being male.

I've never considered myself to be a manly man. For years, I thought to myself, I don't like to hunt, I don't like playing or watching football, and I can barely grow a beard. I thought I was excluded from true manhood, and I often worried if I would ever step into all that manhood demands.

The reality is if you are a male then you are a man. (Wow, that was pretty deep, huh?) It's not your interests, your body shape or size, or your mindsets that make you a man. Instead, you are called to live as a man because God has made you male. So, what does it mean to be a man and how should men who are Christians live their lives?

Every man has some level of insecurity of what it means to be a man. Some have lots of shame and show it; some have shame and do a great job of hiding it. The false things that we believe about manhood are dangerous because they can keep us from our God-given identity. It is important to take the time to uncover what it means to be a man and seek to live out of this identity well.

But where do you start? There are so many definitions and opinions of what a man should be, and even within the Christian church there are controversies about the roles of manhood. The best place to start, I have found, is with Jesus.

Jesus lived a perfect life on Earth. He lived in a physical body that was male and lived as a man in the first century. As our Lord, and one who was fully man as you and I are, Jesus is the best place to start when attempting to answer the question, "What does it mean to be a man?" I want to give you six principles we can learn about Jesus and how he exemplified perfect masculinity to you and I.

Embraced Preparation

Jesus spent a lot of time in preparation season and stewarded the small, not-so-glamorous things in life well. You can see this in how Jesus spent his first thirty years on earth before his ministry started.

As was customary for Jewish boys in the first century, Jesus was likely educated by his father in the home, where he studied and memorized parts of the Torah, the first five books of the Old Testament.[1] It is incredible to notice that once Jesus's ministry began when he was thirty years old, so many of the sermons, lessons, and parables he taught were communicated on the foundation of the scriptures that he learned as a child.

In his early years, Jesus diligently established small habits in his life that helped prepare him for what God was calling him to do later. Per Jewish tradition, Jesus quoted the Shema, that is Deuteronomy 6:4-9; 11:13-21 and Numbers 15:37-41, every morning and every night, helping Jesus to realign his own will to his father's will each day.[2]

Before Jesus's ministry officially began, he began to practice teaching in the temple and learning what the leaders of the temple were saying. At the age of twelve, "Jesus grew in wisdom and stature, and in favor with God and man," Luke tells us (Luke 2:52). In the same way, you can begin to leverage opportunities to practice skills and disciplines to grow you in the direction you think the Lord might be leading you to one day.

Jesus was intentional about stewarding the small things he had been entrusted with well, and men today can do the same. We must seek to be like Jesus and embrace the season of life we find ourselves in. A mark of masculinity is living like Jesus and seeking to be faithful in the present right where God has you.

Recognized Ownership

There was a season in my life where I felt like the Lord was convicting me of a lack of ownership in my life. I wore many hats, such as homeowner, friend, accountability partner, employee, lifting buddy, and church member. But for each, it felt less like I was seizing the opportunity and more like I was floating down a lazy river.

Full ownership looked like me beginning to thank God for the house he had given to me and to begin to invite people into it. It meant me trying to become the best at my role at work and seeking to set goals to measure my success. It looked like me praying for my accountability partner more and showing up to church a little bit earlier to serve as needed and build community. You will have lots of hats that you wear in your life too, but it is important to not expect each of these things to merely serve you.

Jesus did this well. He owned the mission that His father had given him, even to the point of death. Because Jesus knew his identity and who he was, he was able to accept responsibility for the mission that God had given Him. Jesus knew what he was put on earth to do. Luke records Jesus saying, "My food … is to do the will of him who sent me and to finish his work" (Luke 4:34). He established great habits, submitted to the Lord's will often, and surrounded himself in community.

It was through Jesus's personal time with the Lord that he knew it was time to step into his highest mission. On occasion, Jesus would say, "My hour has not yet come" (John 2:4). Jesus knew who he was, he knew the long-term mission, but because of his connection with God he knew that it was not yet time to step into the grand mission of his life.

The small habits in Jesus's life that he established allowed him to accept the responsibility for his purpose and calling. One evening, hours before he was arrested then later to be crucified, Jesus made his way into a garden in the city to pray. It was in this prayer that Jesus resubmitted himself to God's will. Through the habits that Jesus had established when he was a boy, he was able to accept the ownership of the mission that he had.

One of the greatest qualities a man today needs to embody is learning to take ownership of all areas of his life. You and I are accountable to God for knowing the right thing to do. Biblical manhood involves accepting the charge given to us through God's Word to live a life that is honoring to him. It doesn't mean being perfect, but it is crucial that we endeavor to own the place and mission that God has given to us.

Lead Sacrificially

Most Christian men will get married. A crucial responsibility of being a husband is being the leader within your relationship with your wife.

Men are called to be the head of the wife and the family, so it is important to begin learning now about what this means. Scripture tells men, "Love your wives, just as Christ loved the church and gave himself up for her" (Eph. 5:25). This charge to a husband entails the sacrifice of himself for the betterment of his wife.

Jesus is the best person to learn from about living sacrificially. Indeed, Jesus's entire life on earth was centered around the mission of reconciling God's people to God by giving up his own life. This is true sacrificial love.

As Jesus showed sacrificial love for his bride, the church, so we as men need to integrate sacrificial love in our lives too. Jesus loved people with his heart, and he showed this love through his action. In the same way, we must learn to love others well and love our heavenly father deeply, so that out of the overflow of this love may come deeply sacrificial acts.

Showed Honor

Men have a lot of power in the world. Most men abuse this power and fuel their pride by making those weaker than them feel even more weak. But with great physical strength, familial influence, and leadership responsibilities comes a great duty to honor those who are in different positions.

Being a biblical man means to honor those around you, including those who are not always honored in society. Jesus did this well by honoring three different groups of people with whom you and I both need to be certain to honor as well.

First, Jesus honored women. Loving, honoring, and sacrificing for women is something a biblical man must do. It can be tempting to think that women won't understand us, are irrelevant, or are less-than to us, but the truth is both men and women have equal dignity and rights as children of God. Though God made man and woman differently with unique individual qualities, roles, and duties, both men and women are needed for effective ministry work on earth. As Jesus honored many women during his ministry on earth (John 4), we as men should seek to honor women too. Men should never take advantage of any woman, young or old, and should strive to honor women above oneself, seeking to serve them wholeheartedly and to encourage them continuously. We don't do this by compromising on the unique design and duties that God has given specifically to men, but instead we do this because of our design and duty entrusted to us as men from God.

Second, Jesus honored children. As a single guy, I can go weeks without ever talking to someone who is younger than ten years old. A couple of years ago I realized this as a problem and began to get more involved with our children's ministry at my church. As a man, we should seek to be like Jesus in honoring those who are smaller, younger, and more naïve than us. Honoring, protecting, and teaching children is part of being a man. If you do become married one day, likely you will have children and a new mission of discipling, teaching, and leading your young children will take effect. Don't neglect engaging with children now in your single years. Take time now to enjoy the humor and learn the lessons that young believers can teach you.

Finally, Jesus honored other men. Remembering to honor the other men in our life is important. It can be easy to turn to our brothers only when we need something or to think that we can do life on our own and that we don't need guys around us, but honoring the other men God has placed in our lives is important. Through his community of the twelve disciples and others, Jesus did not neglect taking time to be with other God-fearing men. As a man, it is tempting to believe that we can do life alone and that other men will get in our way and slow us down, but the reality is you and I both *need* other men. Being a man means being with other men.

Lived Counterculturally

As I have lived in the South for my entire life, I have been conditioned to be nice no matter what. In the South we only honk if we know the person, and not holding a door open for someone who is still twenty feet away is a crime. But with this comes the natural temptation to always agree with people and comply. However, this can be dangerous.

Recently, God has been showing me the biblical permission that I have to engage in conflict with other people. I've noticed how Jesus has done this in his life too. It is okay to not agree with everyone, and in fact, as Christians, we should often be disagreeing with people who aren't Christians. Indeed, if you have not disagreed with someone recently, this could be a great sign of lack of ownership of what you truly believe about the Christian faith.

Jesus was not afraid to correct false prophets or go toe-to-toe to those who had incorrect theology, and as men, we must be able to do the same thing and defend truth and God's Word. So much of our lives as Christians will be countercultural and we should seek to speak the truth in love to those who oppose us.

You might be thinking, "Aren't women called to be like Jesus, too?" Yes, Christian women are called to be like Christ just as men are. However, men have unique callings and duties that women do not. Men, unlike women, are called to lead their families. Women are not permitted to have elder-level leadership roles in a church like men are. Men have unique responsibilities in both the family and the church that women do not have, and looking to Jesus to learn how to live out these responsibilities is key.

On another important note, we should realize that culture in some senses does help us dictate what men should and should not do. Scripture does tell us that men should not wear a woman's clothing, but in order to define what woman's clothing is, you must look at culture.[3] In Scotland, the men wear kilts, however, in the US, men wear khakis. Decades ago, Mel Gibson wore a kilt in *Braveheart*, and men in the US army in the early 1800s wore kilts during warfare. At large, culture does help to define things like appropriate clothing, and as Christians we should pay attention to this. However, we should never follow culture when it contradicts what is revealed in Scripture about the uniqueness of manhood.

It's not news to you that there is a giant attack on manhood today in our culture. Men are often be praised for being feminine. Many of the movies and TV shows of our day emasculate men and attempt to redefine what it means to be a man. Furthermore, much of modern media tries to make men look incompetent, irrelevant, or unneeded. Often as culture seeks to honor women, they often do so by belittling or downgrading men. Though it is a noble thing to honor women, it should never be done at the expense of the dignity of another. While culture strips men of their dignity and attempts to redefine gender roles, it wonders why there is an increase in divorce, domestic violence, sexual infidelity, abuse, homelessness, and imprisonment. There is surely a link to the lack of raising young boys to be godly men and the deep cultural pain that is noticed today

It is important to go all in on God's calling for you to be a man. Be active in your faith. Steward the small things that God has given you and take ownership of your life. Many guys who are raised in the church believe the lie that they need to do little to nothing with their relationship with God, but this is dangerous.

Nancy Pearcy, in her research on masculinity, found that there is a big difference between nominal Christians and committed Christians. In her study, she compared men who were serious about their faith, who were religiously devout and attended church at least three times per month, with men who claimed to be Christian yet rarely lived devoutly and rarely attended church. Interestingly enough, nominal Christian men have the highest rates of domestic violence compared to any other men in the country, including secular men, while Christian men have proven to show the lowest rates of domestic violence, abuse, and divorce among any other group in the country. Indeed, devout Christian men are proven to be more loving husbands and engaged fathers than secular men or nominal Christians.[4] It is my deep encouragement to you: as a Christian single man, do not conform to the pattern of this world or to the pattern of the typical "Christian" men. Instead go all in on your faith, learning more about and growing in biblical manhood.

It can sometimes feel daunting to consider the various duties of being a man, and shame can quickly creep in and tell us that we are doing it all wrong and that we'll never measure up to the level of true masculinity. But keep pressing on. Continue to watch what Jesus did, and seek to be like him, starting in small ways. The process of conforming to the image of Christ as a man is a long one. Be patient with yourself. Remember that it is not because of anything you have done or will do that will make you more of a son of God. God chose you before the foundations of the world and there is nothing that can separate you from the love God has for his children. Neither is there anything that can make you un-male or not a man. God created you male, and that can't change. The Holy Spirit has chosen you and sealed you with his promise, and that can't change. It is because of this that you get to live life as a son of God.

A Question
Which mark of manhood do you need to focus on in your current season of life?

A Single Shift
Tell God that you would like to stop looking to our culture for ideas about manhood and start looking to the one good man, Jesus. This week, try a habit of reading or listening to the Gospels daily to turn your attention to who Jesus is.

A Prayer
Lord, thank you for making me a man. I recognize that your decision to make me male includes specific responsibilities, duties, and obligations that I must explore and execute. Empower me to take ownership of my life and to honor others including women and children. Help me to learn more from your son about what it means to be a biblical man and conform me into living more like him every day. Amen.

Chapter 5

Single for Life?

Whether you're single for life or will be married, you are the Lord's and should serve the Lord, and your decisions about marriage and singleness should be made in light of this I've often wondered how much money I would have saved up if I collected a dollar every time I was asked "Are you still single?"

Now, I'll say right up front, the question doesn't really bother me. I know that whether I'm single or married, I am the Lord's and will serve him. My decisions about my relationship status will be made in light of this. That said, I'm honored that I have so many people in my life who genuinely care about me. Nonetheless, hearing the question repeatedly for years on end can make you wonder if you're doing life the right way. And I know for me, it made me ask myself if I was really called to a life of singleness.

If you're like me, you might actually be content in your current season of singleness. You see the countless opportunities for growth, service, and dedication to the Lord that seem to be much more difficult to do once you have a family of your own. But if I'm content now in my singleness, does that mean that I should consider being single for the rest of my life?

When I think about what it would be like to live an entire life being single, I think of several people who have done it well. Just take a quick look at scripture and you'll notice many men who lived content single lives and were able to advance the kingdom of God because of it.

Jesus lived about thirty-three years on earth as a single man and during those years radically impacted and changed the trajectory of everyone's life forever. Being like Jesus is one of my goals, so does that mean that I should try to remain single like him too?

What about Paul? Paul, who was likely married at one point, used his later years of singleness to build churches, mentor others, and to change people's lives for eternity. If I want to have a great impact like Paul, does this mean I should remain single forever also? Living a life of singleness is an option for many, but few are called to it.

The Calling of Singleness and the Calling of Marriage

Jesus gives us some insights as he talks about what it means to be called to live a life of singleness. In Matthew 19, Pharisees asked Jesus about the lawfulness of divorce, which in turn prompted Jesus' disciples to question whether it was worth it to become married. The disciples concluded, "If this is the situation between a husband and wife, it is better not to marry" (19:10 NIV). But Jesus' response to them was informing. He said, "Not everyone can accept this word, but only those to whom it has been given" (Matt. 19:11 NIV). Jesus then describes three different categories of those who are called to a life of singleness.

The first category Jesus describes is the "eunuchs who have been so from birth" and the second is the eunuchs "who have been made eunuchs by men" (Matt. 19:12 ESV). A eunuch is a man who does not have the biological components necessary to procreate. Here, Jesus clarifies that there are men who remain single either because of birth defects or due to the rather barbaric means of castration. Thus, these men remain single for a lifetime.

But Jesus continues with a third category, "And there are those who choose to live like eunuchs for the sake of the kingdom of heaven. The one who can accept this should accept it" (Matt. 19:12). While there are some men who have little control over their biological deficiencies and by default remain single, there are also men who have chosen the calling of singleness and live celibate lives (like eunuchs) by choosing not to marry.

Now, this is not me telling you that if you have the slightest desire to live a God-honoring life that you should go and castrate yourself. Instead, I am saying that every man should wrestle with God about whether he is called to a life of marriage or called to a life of singleness.

Paul reaffirms Jesus's teachings in his letter to the Corinthian church. Paul who was not married at the time of writing this letter says, "I wish that all of you were as I am. But each of you has your own gift from God; one has this gift, another has that" (1 Cor. 7:7 NIV). Paul clearly saw great benefit to his relationship status and went so far to suggest his personal preference to others within the church. But he shows us that though singleness is his preference, it is not everyone's calling.

Through Jesus's teaching and Paul's writing, one can infer that choosing to remain single for life or to get married is a choice that every man must make. However, this is not like choosing between Chipotle and Chick-fil-A for dinner. This decision should be made with much care and attention to the Creator's will for your life.

As you make decisions in your life, the motive behind your decision should not go unevaluated. Many people want marriage for the wrong reasons, thinking that marriage will fix their loneliness or secret sins. However, often the needs that a man wants a woman to fill can be found through Christ alone. The ultimate goal as a Christian is not to become married or even to remain single; instead the goal is to abide in Christ, live a life of surrender to God's will, and remain obedient to him so that he may receive maximum glory. It is the mark of a biblical man to choose to submit to God's will rather than one's own and to wrestle with God on what his calling is.

Paul continues in his letter to the church, "But if they cannot control themselves, they should marry, for it is better to marry than to burn with passion" (1 Cor. 7:9 NIV). Paul is not commanding those who are consumed with lust to get married to the first person that they see. Instead, Paul was writing this to a group of Christians where many engaged couples were choosing to not marry because they thought sex was wrong (1 Cor. 7:1). The decision of getting married should be made carefully and with the right motives. I've had to do this. And just like you would do these things as you try to figure out any other calling in life, you must discern where God is calling you in life as it relates to relationship status.

The calling of singleness is an incredibly noble calling. Those who are called to a biblical life of singleness will never marry, never have sex, and never have children. They choose, rather, to devote their lives to the advancement of the gospel message here on earth. This is a remarkable token of sacrifice and dedication to abandon the natural desires and functions of the human body to serve the kingdom of God at a greater capacity.

Singleness is *for* God completely. In other words, singleness exists not to become more available to yourself but more available to God. When you are single, whether you are called to a season or a life of singleness, God will be the banner of your life.

God allows many men to remain single for life so that he can accomplish some of his greatest works. I have found in my own season of singleness that God can be more demanding than a relationship can be. There is a holy agenda attached to every single man, and you might be called on, demanded of, and asked of more than many other men ever will be.

Paul tells us, "A married man is concerned about the affairs of this world—how he can please his wife" (1 Cor. 7:33 NIV). This is the reality of those who choose marriage. Marriage will prompt a different set of demands and responsibilities than those who are living a life of singleness. Think for a moment about the demands that marriage brings. You have a wife you are responsible to lead. You must challenge her, listen to her, provide for her, and care for her. And think about the demands a family has too. You, as the father, are tasked with disciplining, protecting, and providing for an array of needs for each of your children.

The agenda of demands that a family can place on a man is quite extensive, but the agenda of God is even greater. And as a single man, you would have the platform and the capability to carry out the works of God that many men simply do not have time for. Paul says it this way: "I would like you to be free from concern. An unmarried man is concerned about the Lord's affairs—how he can please the Lord" (1 Cor. 7:32 NIV). The life of a godly single man is a life that revolves around the heart and will of God.

Just as many men want to get married for the wrong reasons, many men also desire to stay single for the wrong reasons too. It might be because they don't want the commitment and sacrifice marriage brings. They might enjoy the financial gains that comes from not having a family to support. Or they believe their sexual desires can be met through masturbation and one-night stands. But these are faulty motives for remaining single. God is clear that if a man is called to a life of singleness, that calling exists for the sake of the kingdom of God alone.

God's Supply for Singleness

I used to wonder how a single man could reap some of the same benefits God gives to men who are married. Does the single man just miss out on the prayers his wife would be praying over him? Must he burn with sexual passion? Will he be more idle with the free time he has, thus leading him into temptation and perhaps selfishness as he pursues his own desires and motives?

One must remember that God will always provide the tools you need to carry out your mission and calling. When God calls a man to be single, he provides the means to live a holy and fruitful life. If God blesses a man with marriage, God will honor this and, through the power of the Holy Spirit, give you the ability to sacrificially love your wife.

Single men can also rely on the power of the Holy Spirit in hopes of having his spiritual, physical, and biological needs met for him. There will be struggles, temptations, and challenges that he will need to work through for both the single and married man, but God will provide the strength one needs to live a God-honoring life.

As a single guy, I've experienced this before. Even though I believe I am not called to a life of single living, as a guy who is currently single, I have seen, through the ministry of the Holy Spirit, my emotional, physical, and spiritual needs met without a woman to meet them. It's a complete fulfillment that is only made available and only discovered through the indwelling of the Spirit within you. In the season of singleness God has called you into, he will make known to you the ability to live life in modern culture as a single man while producing fruit, making a difference, and being content.

Singleness Is a Gift

Whether singleness is for life or for a season, everyone must realize that singleness is a gift from God. It is not the second best, and the men who are single did not mess up more than the men who are married. It simply means God has an individual and unique calling on the single man's life and often God is doing a work in a through a man more than anyone can see or notice.

On the other hand, becoming a husband and leading a family is a noble calling but it is not better than or worse than the call to a life of singleness. Both singleness and marriage must be honored as statuses of life that God uses to build his church in unique ways.

For those who are not called to life of singleness, we must constantly ask ourselves, "How am I supporting the men and women around me who are indeed called to singleness?" We cannot allow ourselves to cast judgement on these brothers and sisters, and we must faithfully work to promote the wellbeing and flourishing of these members of our spiritual family. Instead of trying to solve an unbroken problem by attempting to set up men and women called to singleness with a potential spouse, we should seek to understand the unique needs and requests of our brothers and sisters who are stewarding the Lord's calling.

For those who are called to a life of singleness, ask yourself, "How I can serve the kingdom of God with the extra time that I have, including those who are married?" Challenge yourself to spend time with men who are husbands and to learn what it means to be married and have children.

Looking at the greater landscape of men in the global church, I believe that most men are called to marriage one day, and it's likely that most men reading this book will be committed to a wife one day as well. After all, how could we sustain generations without the procreation that comes as a fruit of being married? But so many struggle to understand their current season of life right now and how it ties into the future seasons of life they will find themselves in.

If you're single right now, the best thing you can be doing is becoming concerned about the Lord's affairs and you can please the Lord as Paul encourages us to do (1 Cor. 7:32). Make this your top priority. Do this above looking for a suitable wife even if you think you are called to marriage one day. God has placed you in this season of singleness right now to accomplish some great works through you.

Your identity that you have rooted in God will help activate you to a life of service and dedication to the kingdom of God. Continue to seek to find out what God says about your identity in his Word and spend time reinforcing those truths in your mind. Your understanding of the significance of singleness will stem from the ultimate understanding of who you are as a son of God.

A Question
Do you currently idolize marriage or singleness? How do you view each calling as significant roles within Christ's church?

A Single Shift
If you have never considered whether you are called to a life of singleness, take some time to ask God whether that is what he wants for you. If you have considered it but don't feel any clarity, ask a pastor or mentor to help you think through the biblical teaching as it relates to your life.

A Prayer
Lord, thank you for creating me and allowing me to live life during such a time as this. I confess to you my discontent of the season of life that you have placed me, whether past or present, and I ask that you cultivate a heart of gratitude within me for where you have placed me. Teach me to be anxious about what you are anxious about and use my single status as nothing short of an opportunity to influence others for your kingdom. Amen.

PART TWO
Find Freedom

Chapter 6

Let Freedom Ring

Singleness affords you an opportunity for freedom. No, I'm not talking about freedom from a wife and the opportunity to live up the bachelor lifestyle. What I mean is that your single years are a unique time to grasp the promise of freedom from sin through Christ Jesus. To the world, this will look ridiculous, but to your future this is absolutely necessary.

Whatever God's reason for giving you this season of singleness, and whatever his purpose is for your future, he has made at least this much known: "It is God's will that you should be sanctified: that you should avoid sexual immorality; that each of you should learn to control your own body in a way that is holy and honorable" (1 Thess. 4:3–4 NIV). In other words, God wants you to pinpoint and work through the toxic thinking, sexual brokenness, and secret sins plaguing your life right now. Your single years are an opportunity to find freedom from these sins before they have the opportunity to threaten your servant leadership of your wife in marriage.

Finding this freedom means pursuing holiness and seeking to grow in the kind of character that God desires for his children. When we pursue holiness, we become more like the person of Jesus Christ. Pursuing holiness involves growing in your awareness of sins in your life, eliminating habits that may lead to sin, and replacing these habits with actions that yield to you becoming more like Christ. Doing this won't be easy, and it will be countercultural. But it will be better for you, your friends, and your future family in the long term. Here's are some reasons why you should focus working through your greatest struggles now.

Concealing Sin Collapses Your Future

It's impossible to flourish while living a sinful lifestyle. James makes this clear when he writes, "Sin, when it is full-grown, gives birth to death" (1:15 NIV). For most people, it's the sins they never reveal to anyone that are silently killing them on the inside. You know what you do is wrong, but the guilt and shame you face is too much to bear and you're launched back into the cycle of sin after you promised yourself you'd never do it again.

Concealing sin is second nature to us. As soon as Adam and Eve sinned, they hid from God. And we do the same. We believe the lie that we can fix things on our own and that we are better off if no one knows the depth to which we struggle. But Proverbs tells us differently, "Whoever conceals their sins does not prosper, but the one who confesses and renounces them finds mercy" (28:13 NIV). Since God's Word is true, then it's true we won't go far if we conceal our sins.

Marriage Will Not Fix the Problem

For years, I believed that if I just started dating someone and got married, then I would be free from all my darkest sins. For years I believed a lie.

The truth is: what is minimized now will be maximized later. The same temptations you have now will not evaporate once you get married. In fact, you might even face even stronger, darker, and more enticing temptations once you're married.

It's crucial that you begin to learn holy and biblical ways to fight against your greatest temptations in your weakest times. A friend used to tell me, no matter how far along the road of life you go, the ditch is always the same distance away. You'll be tempted for the rest of your life to turn to fleshly and worldly habits, so it is critical that you learn how to respond to these temptations now.

Who you are today foreshadows who you will be when you are married. A wedding won't change that. Only God can change that as you actively seek him for freedom from sin. So right now, in your single years, you have the chance to reshape how you handle these temptations and how you approach your weaknesses.

The Quest for Freedom is Lifelong

Before I lure you in with a dangling carrot in front of your face, you should know that the pursuit of holiness is lifelong. You won't be able to fix everything before you get married, and you will (hopefully) always be wrestling with the Lord about your sins.

This realization hit me hard, because I am an achiever and I like to get things done. My counselor called me out one day when he noticed how frustrated I was that I still faced the same temptations to sin. He reminded me that, even though I can exercise self-control in response to temptations, I can't stop temptations from coming or choose which ones will confront me.

God allows you to go through temptations and hardships so that he can teach you some of his greatest lessons just as he has done with many of the characters we read about throughout the Bible (see Psalm 91:14-16). God will use all your temptations to test you and He will use all your trials to teach you.

As you dive into reframing your single years to find freedom through a pursuit of holiness, your ability to do two things will determine the progress you make.

First, coming close to God. You cannot find freedom if you do not know God. That's why the first part of this book focused on uncovering who you are as you abide in Christ. The depth of your relationship with Christ has a direct correlation with how well you break free from the past and say no to the temptations of the world. Pursuing holiness means pursuing God. There is no substitute for your relationship with God.

Second, your progress toward holiness is attached to the boundaries you set in place. The things you cut out of your life, the people you stop hanging out with, the apps you delete, and the thoughts you stop dwelling on will accelerate your journey toward godliness.

I'll warn you up front: finding freedom is hard. You might be tempted to quit, and you could desire to go back to your old ways. But remind yourself that it is the harder things in the short run that lead to flourishing in the long run. The writer of Hebrews said it this way, "No discipline seems pleasant at the time, but painful. Later on, however, it produces a harvest of righteousness and peace for those who have been trained by it" (Heb. 12:11 NIV). Are you ready to use your single years for painful discipline so that later you may reap a harvest of godly living?

A Question
What is a struggle in your life that you would like to seek freedom from while you are single?

A Single Shift
Spend time thinking about what your life would be like if you were to find freedom from some of the sins in your life. Think about the joy it would be for you to look like Christ more. When you are tempted to go back to old patterns, remind yourself of this joy you are seeking.

A Prayer
Lord, thank you for the opportunity I have in this life to grow and become more sanctified. Help me to pursue holiness so that I may live more like Christ each day. Reveal my sins to me and allow your community of believers through the Holy Spirit to help me in this quest for freedom. Amen.

Chapter 7

Lust

It's no surprise that one of the biggest hurdles that most men struggle with is sexuality. I want to spend a few chapters here getting into the weeds of lust, porn, masturbation, and sex and offering practical help in these areas.

So many guys get discouraged when they see an attractive person and cannot get past the temptation to lust after them. I know I have. It can feel like you are running on a treadmill, because it feels as if you can never kill the act of lust. And it can be just flat out annoying.

No matter where you go, you are guaranteed to see people who you find to be attractive. The attractive people are not the problem. The problem is how you *respond* in your mind to people you find attractive.

As you think about lust, it is important to think about what lust signals to us. What is going on beneath the surface? Ultimately, lust is taking what was originally designed for good and twisting it for evil. This happens because of the effects of sin. You see, you and I are designed to appreciate beauty. God created man to pursue woman, so it makes sense that a man would be able to lock in and appreciate a woman's beauty and experience sexual desire. However, sin has powerfully twisted our good desire of appreciating beauty into idolatry, lust, and abuse.

It's easy to overlook lust and write it off as okay since no one could ever know what you are thinking inside your head, but it's often the small compromises that lead to the greatest destruction. Allowing lust to set up shop in our minds will cause us to compromise on obedience to a greater degree down the road. Lust affects you more deeply than you think, and it has an effect on your future pursuit of holiness. Jesus warns us, "The eye is the lamp of the body. If your eyes are healthy, your whole body will be full of light. But if your eyes are unhealthy, your whole body will be full of darkness" (Matt. 6:22–23 NIV). What you do with your eyes doesn't just stop with your eyes. As Jesus says, it has the power to affect your entire body. Lust may seem small, but its effects are huge.

When we lust, we disrespect the person we lust after and God. When you gaze, stare, or fantasize, you abandon the truth about someone's identity as a person created in God's image and you make them into an object for your own sexual gratification. Lust destroys, degrades, and disregards the God-given honor of an image-bearing child of God.

Lust was prevalent during Jesus's time on earth—so much so, that Jesus preached on the topic of lust. In a sermon, Jesus said, "But I say to you that everyone who looks at a woman with lustful intent has already committed adultery with her in his heart" (Matt. 5:28 ESV). Here Jesus takes the issue of lust and elevates it to equaling the abominable sin of adultery. This is a massive statement. Jesus says that lust *equals* adultery. Why is this?

The answer is simple. Jesus calls Christians to live a life of complete holiness that starts with the eyes, mind, and heart. The goal is not to just not commit adultery; it is also to keep everything about you pure and holy. Think about it this way, if Jesus had not equated lust to adultery, then you and I would be free to lust and indulge in sexual passion so long as we did not commit adultery. But Jesus desires total heart change from his followers.

Jesus knows that small acts of lust lead to greater and worse sins later on. As a follower of Christ, you and I are called to a life of complete holiness, and that means being conscious of where we look.

Now, as we consider Jesus's words, it is interesting to me how Jesus did not say, "Whoever looks at a woman has already committed adultery," but instead he says, "whoever looks at a woman *with lustful intent*," communicating that it is the lustful thought in our minds that is the problem. So just seeing a woman who is attractive is not the problem, because, indeed, you will continue to see attractive people for the rest of your life. Instead, it is the second look, the place your mind goes, or how you engage with that person that gives birth to the sin.

This is a liberating thought! It is okay to acknowledge that someone is attractive, but it's not okay to lust, crave, or fantasize over that person. You're not messed up because you notice that a woman is very attractive; that is a normal experience.

It is also important to note that you are not messed up if you are being *tempted* to lust. Remember, Jesus himself was tempted, and he lived a life without sin. In the same way Jesus said no to temptation, so you and I must make the difficult decision to say no to the temptation to lust.

I say this to you because I know so many guys get trapped in the cycle of shame about seeing attractive people or being tempted. It is okay for both these things to be present in your life! What is not okay is giving into sin. Let the temptations you have draw you closer to God. You will never stop seeing attractive people, nor will you ever stop being tempted, so don't get caught in the shame that we naturally reap on ourselves.

So how do you fight lust? Well, Scripture is clear about how to respond to the enticing sexual temptations of our day. And the good news is, Scripture doesn't give us a complicated prescription on how to respond to our burning temptations; it's actually pretty simple.

Flee

So many guys who I talk to get discouraged about their desires to give into lust as they continue to look at images and put themselves in places where they see attractive people. Scripture tells us to do it differently. Paul tells us simply to "*flee* from sexual immorality" (1 Cor. 6:18 NIV). Run away! When we are tempted with lust, we are to run! Sprint! Eagerly abandon the situation we are in and flee! This is the opposite of lingering over a person, image, or fantasy. Get as far away from these temptations as you can when they come.

Renew

Because we are such sinful creatures living on a broken planet, we will constantly have to train our mind to think purer and more holy thoughts rather than the wicked and conceited thoughts we naturally enjoy. Scripture calls this a "renewing of the mind." Romans 12:2 tells us that to be transformed, we must renew our mind. This means we recognize our evil and impure thoughts and then make the conscience effort to replace these thoughts with the truth of scripture (see 2 Cor. 10:4-6).

Trust

Temptations attempt to present crystal-clear visions of the world you could you be living in if you just gave into that temptation. Therefore, the opposite of diving into a temptation is living by faith and being obedient to what God has called you to do. Faith is something that cannot be seen; it requires full surrender and trust to walk forward even if you cannot see where your foot will land (see Hebrews 11:1). Living by faith is the opposite of living by the desires of your flesh.

You must choose to live in faith that God's way is better for you. Obedience and doing things God's way will not make sense to you on the front end, but it is better for you in the long run. When you are tempted to indulge in lust, you must remind yourself of the commands of God and your personal commitment you have to order your life around his designs and desires for your life rather than your own. Scripture encourages us, "This is love for God: to keep his commands. And his commands are not burdensome, for everyone born of God overcomes the world. This is the victory that has overcome the world, even our faith" (1 John 5:3-4). Trust that God's way is better and order your life accordingly.

A Question

What are some of the potential consequences in life that could occur if I do not fight the desire to lust?

A Single Shift

Consider the triggers (people, places, moods, etc.) that have sent you into a lustful mindset. Write down the most significant triggers and consider how you might respond to these triggers with prayer—for example, praying before entering an empty house, or praying for the good of a person you are tempted to lust after.

A Prayer

God, I thank you for designing me with capacity to appreciate your creation and beauty. As sin fills this earth, I recognize that my appreciation of beauty has become twisted and often leads me to sin. Lord, would you put a desire in my heart to fight the temptation to lust and would you help me to flee, renew my mind, and to trust your Word and your commandments? I pray that you create a body filled with light as I strive to keep my eyes pure. Thank you, Lord. Amen.

Chapter 8

The Itch for Intimacy

I am extremely allergic to poison ivy. I could tell you about the time as a kid where I spend hours building the coolest fort in the woods, only to realize two days later that my entire fort was built out of poison ivy leaves. I could tell you about the time that I played with poison ivy vines in the winter because I thought that, like other plants, poison ivy was dead in the winter. I could even tell you about the time where I might have just accidentally picked the wrong leaves in the woods when I was going number two on a hiking trip. Yeah, that one wasn't fun at all.

If you're allergic to poison ivy, you know what the itch is like. It's different from a typical bug bite or rash. Poison ivy leaves behind a never-ending, burning irritation. It goes deep into the skin and is a constant itch that can never quite be satisfied. Even when you scratch it (and you're not supposed to!), the relief comes for a second, but then the itch roars back to life again.

You don't have to be allergic to poison ivy to experience this unending itch in your own life. The odds are that you have likely experienced something similar as it relates to your desire for sexual intimacy. Your burning for intimacy has led you to looking at more porn than you ever would have imagined and giving into masturbation time and time again. You have the desire to look at something, so you satisfy the desire by indulging in what you want, only to realize temporary that relief was.

Every human is hardwired for intimacy. The word *intimacy* often alludes to sexual encounters, but I want to talk about intimacy as a more broad concept and define it as a close relationship with another person or with God. Every human has these desires. Everyone has a desire to know God deeply (see Ecclesiastes 3:11) and a desire to be close with others—not just a spouse, but family and friends in authentic community.

The bad news is as we live on a sinful planet, our desires for closeness to God and to others has become twisted and thwarted and we often look to satisfy these desires of intimacy through sexual acts. Within a marriage, sexual acts are one good expression of a particular kind of intimacy. But when someone makes an effort to satisfy their broad need for intimacy through sexual acts outside of marriage, this becomes sin. Ultimately, it cannot satisfy this need.

Porn is one of the most prevalent concerns facing men today. The cycle is hard to break. You can spend hours looking at porn, then experience shame just minutes after turning it off. Then, you make a promise to yourself that you will never do such a horrible thing again, but before long you are watching it again. It's gross and it's fun at the same time. Before looking at it, it's the only thing on the planet that you want; yet afterwards, your guilt takes over and you crave anything but.

The global pornography industry is booming and brings in revenue north of $97 billion each year.[5] In the United States, the porn industry yields $12–14 billion and makes up 20 percent of e-commerce sales.[6] This successful industry incentivizes companies to continue to produce content in the hopes of yielding a profit. Porn is more accessible than ever before, so it is important for you to take time to understand the causes that lead you to looking at porn and develop disciplines in your life to end this habit.

The word *porn* or *pornography* is derived from the Greek word *porneia*, which means "sexual immorality." Thus, we can make the inference that any sort of lust, viewing of sexually explicit images, and sexual encounters with others are a form of porn.

Porn is a major problem for many reasons. For starters, pornography, coupled with masturbation, completely rewires a man's brain and changes the way he thinks.[7] It causes men to turn women into sexual objects while at the same time encouraging a man's own isolation. Its Hollywood-style scenes portray sex in an unrealistic way that could cause a man to have unrealistic expectations for sex within marriage.

Porn is a massive problem, and in order to really "fix" the problem of porn in your life, you will need to start with the root issue. So many men experience shame after looking at an explicit image or masturbating to pornography, and this causes them to avoid thinking about what it is that keeps leading them back to this very habit. It is important that we dig deep and consider what is truly at the heart of these desires.

We need to remember that it is in fact God who created sex, not man. God designed sex to be an pleasure-filled act between a husband and a wife and to be an act of worship to him. Better yet, God made sex as a means to reproduce in order to create more image-bearers who could populate the earth and worship God. God is not surprised at our love for sex, women, or beauty. Indeed, it is he who created them.

The problem is that because sin entered the world, we now wrestle with these good desires within the context of a broken and sinful planet. Thus, many of our desires, though they are God-given and good, have been twisted and distorted by Satan. Since Satan does not have the power to create anything, his strategic attack is to twist good desires into evil acts. We must now take special care to preserve these good desires within their holy contexts rather than using these desires to satisfy ourselves and give into sin.

Understanding this helps profoundly with the shame struggle. I have talked to dozens of men who agree that after looking at porn and masturbating, the feeling of shame looms intensely over them, and the fog of shame cripples their ability to enjoy the blessing of the gospel truth and the freedom of Christ. But reminding ourselves that God originally gave us these desires and the thirst for sex gives us a proper view of the created order and empowers us to take dominion over the temptations of the flesh.

Men turn back to pornography over and over again because it promises to satisfy their desire of intimacy. There is a sense of belonging that comes with looking at porn. As I stated earlier, men and women will always have the desire to be close to other people, and so often men will try to satisfy these desires by looking at porn.

Please hear this: God created you as an intimate person to crave intimacy and enjoy intimacy to its fullest. You're hard-wired for it, and the truth is every man has the desire to love others and to be loved. The reason men turn to porn is because we seek and crave intimacy. Porn often offers the most intense feelings of intimacy that a man has ever experienced—despite the fact that there is no real intimacy, because you're not interacting with a real person.

I learned this in college when I noticed that I often faced temptations right after church, or when I had been around people who made me feel loved and cared for. The desire and need for intimacy never dissolves, but in this sinful world, we have trained ourselves to satisfy this itch in the wrong ways.

If men want to overcome porn, men must learn to address the real issue of the heart. The heart longs for intimacy. A man must learn to satisfy this intimate itch or deep desire. Ultimately, as a single guy, the cure lies in seeking a deep and loving relationship with God, with other Christian men, and in appropriate settings with Christian women. A fulfilling, ongoing, dynamic relationship between a son of God and his heavenly Father is the ultimate cure for the constant itch for intimacy. And God meets with his sons through other sons and through sisters in Christ. Cultivating a life where you enjoy God and his people in authentic ongoing relationship becomes the greatest strategy in defeating your struggle against pornography.

Think about a husband who might be tempted to cheat on his wife. If a husband decides to dedicate himself fully to his wife, his desires to cheat on her will likely decrease. But if he fails to cultivate a nurturing and loving relationship with her, he might be more inclined to an affair. It is because of a man's love for his wife that he opts to not cheat on her. In fact, it is with great joy that he honors his wife and enjoys sex with her. He does not say, "Darn, I guess I just won't cheat on my wife tonight, since I'm not supposed to." No, instead the intimacy he's created with his wife drives away outside temptations.

Indeed, it is almost always better to run toward something than to run from something. So many men know pornography is wrong, but they try to fight this struggle with the wrong strategy. They think about the hundreds of ways to say no to porn and the boundaries that must be put in place instead of running to something better. Focus on running to God and to your relationships with other believers rather than running from porn. Allowing God to truly satisfy the desire you have for intimacy is a much better strategy than just telling yourself no repeatedly every time you have the thought of looking at porn.

Overcoming porn comes down to your willingness to do the hard work and go deeper in your relationship with God and with others. And yes, I did say hard work. This looks like choosing to spend time with God in prayer when you have the strongest temptation to look at porn. When you're alone and tempted to look at something, this looks like going to the bedroom, getting on your knees, and choosing to spend time with God in conversation. This looks like going for a walk and talking out loud to God. This means opening your Bible instead of your computer when you have an urge. This is hard work and nothing in you will want to do this when you want to look at porn.

You must train yourself to seek satisfaction for your desire for intimacy with God rather than with porn. Spoiler alert: the desire for intimacy will never go away. Thus, for the rest of your life, you must make conscious efforts and intentional decisions to satisfy these intimate desires appropriately.

Spending time with other people is also a great way to refocus these intimate desires. Ultimately, your desires must be satisfied by God, but God uses his people to help you feel known, seen, and like you belong. When you have the deep desire to look at porn or to go back to a sinful place where you have found intimacy before, flee from these temptations and find people you can be with. Call a friend. Invite someone over. Go meet someone for dinner. Facilitate something that will allow you to enjoy communion with other brothers and sisters in Christ.

We can't take this lightly, as we are part of the body of Christ that exists for service to his kingdom. I encourage you to be ruthless about eliminating the habit of porn in your life. Use the steps outlined in the prior to chapter to help you escape the cycle of trying to find contentment and joy in explicit images. As we consider the damaging effects of porn and how it traps you and holds you back, it will also be important to understand the effects that the act of masturbation has on your, your brain, and your relationships with others. To that we now turn.

A Question
Have you considered building an intimate relationship with God before? How might doing so effect your relationship with sin?

A Single Shift
Next time you have an urge to look at porn, take five minutes to evaluate what your body and mind are truly desiring. Pray, and tell God how you are being tempted and what you are desiring.

A Prayer
Lord, I recognize that I am a sinner and am in desperate need of your grace and forgiveness. You are holy and righteous, and I desire to be like you. Would you please highlight to me the ways in which my heart desires intimacy and empower me to choose to cultivate intimacy with you rather than in something worldly. God, I pray that the intimacy that I experience with you would reshape my life and conform me more into the image of Christ. Amen.

Chapter 9

Irritating the Itch

I told you earlier about my unfortunate natural inclination in life to attract poison ivy to my skin. I can't tell you how many times I have had poison ivy, and each time is just as bad as the time before. The thing with poison ivy is that you want the rash to dry out over time. If it doesn't try out, then it could get worse and spread to other parts of your body. There was one time when I made the mistake of using skin lotion to moisturize the poison ivy rash that I had. Yikes! Instead of my rash disappearing, the moisturizer boosted the ivy and the itch became more inflamed. That was not fun! Maybe I'll write a book one day on all the things I have learned about poison ivy.

As men continue on their journeys toward finding freedom from sexual issues plaguing their past and present, it is important to talk about a habit that so many men do that inflames their itch for intimacy and sexual desires and in turn paralyzes men. Masturbation is one of the greatest struggles that the men I talk to today experience. For some guys, masturbation continues to be an issue even after they have freedom from pornography. For some, the main sexual struggle in their life is masturbation, but they cannot break the weekly, daily, or even hourly routine of this act.

As we consider masturbation, we must let God's Word inform us on what to make of this act. The Bible doesn't address masturbation directly at all, though it may be alluded to in some places. While it doesn't address specifically whether it is a sin or not, it does inform us how to order our lives and uphold a sexual ethic as a disciple of Christ.

Paul encourages believers to live a pure life and to not let there be "even a hint of sexual immorality, or of any kind of impurity…because these are improper for God's holy people" (Eph. 5:3 NIV). We know that sexual acts are intended by God to be pleasureful and enjoyed by a man and woman who are married. Any sexual acts that are conducted outside of God's design for marriage is a sin and is an action that easily will have its own consequences.

It can be tempting to think that because no one else is involved in the act of masturbation, and if you can do it without lustful images in your minds, then masturbation is fine to do and indeed not a sin. But this doesn't make it right. Even if you do authentically keep your mind free from lustful thoughts and images, you are still taking a sexual act out of the right context and using it for your own personal enjoyment. Masturbation is indeed a sin, and your chance of overcoming this habit in your life will increase when you begin to address it as such.

Let's think a little bit more about this habit and the effects it is having on your life. Orgasm produces one of the most powerful chemical experiences you will have in your brain. It is a fireworks display of neurochemicals. And as you repeat this habit, neural pathways are established that encourage continual indulgence.

One of the most powerful chemicals that is released when you have an organism is dopamine. This hormone activates or enhances your reward circuitry in your mind. It's the "feel good" feeling that comes when you have an organism. And because dopamine also assists your brain with memory, when you are triggered sexually, dopamine reminds you have responded to this trigger in the past. If you've responded to sexual passions in the past by masturbating, dopamine is right there to remind you to respond the same way. As dopamine assists in the cravings for future orgasm, this "drug" becomes highly addictive.

Additionally, when you masturbate, oxytocin is released in your brain. Oxytocin is a bonding chemical. Whatever you are looking at in the moment, oxytocin helps you to bond to that thing. This is incredibly powerful. No matter what you are looking at when you give into this, oxytocin is there to help you super-glue yourself to that object, person, or image. Every time you indulge, you continually bond and attach yourself to the thing you are looking at whatever the object may be.

Another important dynamic to this conversation is your testosterone level. Testosterone in men is produced throughout the day, but when a man is stimulated sexually, the body produces this chemical in even greater amounts. These greater amounts lead to a chemical imbalance in men which causes men to sexualize people and objects more often and increases their desire for intimacy.[8] Sound familiar?

There are many other chemicals in your brain that are released when you have an orgasm, but understanding what the powers of dopamine, oxytocin, and testosterone are will help you in your fight against this unwanted habit.

A man seeking to overcome the desire to give into the sin of masturbation must examine the triggers in his life that encourage him to do this act. For some, there are physical triggers, like walking into an empty house, getting into the shower, lying in bed, or changing clothes. There are also emotional triggers that can lead a man to give into this sin—things like feeling neglected in community, feeling shameful about one's body, failing at a task, getting rejected, being insecure about masculinity, or feeling stressed.

What's important to notice is that many of the triggers you experience are normal, everyday things that are hard to avoid. Seeing an attractive person, being rejected, or changing clothes are all things that will likely happen to you every day of your life. So the problem resides not so much with these triggers. Instead, it's in how you deal with the temptation to sin when you experience one of these triggers.

These things became triggers in your life because you have trained yourself to respond to these physical and emotional states by stimulating yourself. Over time, you have led yourself to believe that the best way to cope with these experiences is by sexually gratifying yourself.

Your brain is highly bendable and moldable, and a lot the triggers and attractions you have exist because you have trained your brain to crave these things. Each time you give into this sin, the intense release of the dopamine, testosterone, and oxytocin fuel the ability to create what are called "neuropathways" in your brain. In the same way a trail in the woods is established by walking the trail over and over again, your brain creates trails, or pathways, when you do an activity over and over again. This is what creates addiction. You might be so used to masturbating after seeing someone attractive, but that is because you have trained your brain to do this. You might be prompted to give into this sin as soon as you get home from work each day because you have trained your brain to think this way. The physical and emotional triggers that lead you to self-gratification are trained ways of thinking and must be undone.

So how do we break this cycle of giving into self-gratification every time we face these triggers? We must do it the same way that we taught ourselves *to* sin when we face a trigger. We must learn to channel these triggers to something else that can give better and longer-lasting relief than masturbation can.

You must take the time in your single years to notice and describe the triggers that are leading you into sin. By noticing these, you are then able to address them. I wish I could list all the different triggers that could be crippling you, but because sin is so evasive and has affected each of our lives differently, this would turn into a very long book!

Once you notice these triggers, your long-term goal should be to seek to find intimacy with God any time one of these triggers comes up in your mind. That sounds pretty far-fetched doesn't it? You might be saying, "Sam, how on earth am I supposed to channel my insecurities of my body and my feelings of rejection to God?" Many guys say this. And they have used masturbation as a coping mechanism to numb the pain or hurt experienced.

But instead, you must order your life to turn your deep desires for masturbation into an authentic and trusting relationship with God. Just as you've done this with porn and sexually explicit images, you too must learn to turn to God in these areas of life.

Think about what some of the triggers for giving into masturbation could be telling you.

If you do this act because you are insecure about your own body, does this mean you need to spend time with the Creator of your body and ask him to give you a better approach to yourself?

If you give into this every time you are rejected, what an opportunity this is to find complete acceptance by your own heavenly Father!

If you give into masturbation every day you see an attractive woman (which will likely be every day for the rest of your life!), this might mean you need to spend time asking God to help you see these women as image bearers and pray for these women.

Maybe you give into this sin when you're lonely, so how can you find relationship, conversation, and fulfillment with God through prayer or talking to him instead?

If you give into this right before bed every night, how can you reorder this time to enjoy God and his company instead?

The triggers of this sin reveal many of the wounds that we have. However, we can be hope-filled as we think about bringing God into these wounds and giving these insecurities to him.

Growth in resisting the temptation of porn and masturbation happens when we recognize the deep need for intimacy that we all have. As opposed to channeling this desire for intimacy through sexually explicit images and the act of masturbation, we must learn to channel these intimate desires to our heavenly Father. Our own sexual stimulation—and, in fact, even that of a future spouse—will never provide us with the satisfaction that we so deeply desire. We must die to self and be active men who choose to kneel before God rather than click away on the computer for the fulfillment of our needs. There is nothing easy about it, but it is the call to us as Christian disciples. God is truly the only one who can satisfy our itch for intimacy.

A Question

What are some of the physical and emotional triggers that lead you to masturbation?

A Single Shift

During a temptation to seek self-pleasure, boldly get on your knees before

God and tell him how you feel and what you are experiencing. Seek to find closeness and intimacy with God rather than yourself.

A Prayer

Lord, thank you for creating me as a sexual being. I notice that sin has corrupted so many good things including my desire for intimacy. I confess that I have sought to find pleasure and intimacy in places other than in you. Holy Spirit, please illuminate the triggers that cause me to give into this sin and give me the courage, strength, and willingness to run toward you when I experience an intimate urge. Thank you for designing me with great complexity and wonder. Amen.

Chapter 10

The Eight As

In no way are men limited to struggling only with sexual sins. Through countless breakfasts, lunches, dinners, phone calls, FaceTimes, walks, long drives, and plane rides I've taken with other guys, I've noticed that there are a significant number of issues that men struggle with. Men are complex, and sin has spread its tentacles in creative ways to paralyze men.

I want to spend a little bit of time unpacking a few of the common issues that I have seen young Christian men struggle with. I want to encourage you to read through this entire chapter even if you know that you don't struggle with one of the particular issues. Learning about what other men might struggle with will allow you to be a more faithful brother in Christ and might even encourage you in your own quest for freedom.

As we continue to reframe singleness as an opportunity to find freedom, let's turn now to what I call "The Eight As" to dig up, rake out, and work through some of the biggest struggles plaguing your life. Instead of offering a single shift and prayer prompt at the end of this chapter, I'll offer thoughtful questions to ask yourself concerning each of these topics.

Anger

I worked as a camp counselor one summer during college, and if you've worked camp before, you know the days are long, the campers can be challenging, and sometimes it can even be hard to get along with your leadership. One night after camp, the other counselors and our leaders decided to play a game of pickup basketball. It wasn't long into the game when a lot of the guys were beginning to show intense anger toward one another and began to use curse words and throw elbows. We quickly realized that these guys weren't angry about the basketball game that was taking place; rather, they were surfacing some of the anger they had toward one another and toward the camp. I learned a lot working at camp this summer, but it was in this moment when I realized that anger often reveals something in us beneath the surface.

If you struggle with frequently becoming angry, you likely need to stop and examine what is going on in your heart. You might be hurt at something that happened days, weeks, or even years ago. Maybe you're frustrated at your lack of control or the expectations that were not met.

Oftentimes anger surfaces when you are trying to conceal secret sins and you harbor pride. When someone or something threatens the kingdom you are building for yourself, you lash out. Or you might get angry because that is simply how you were taught to respond to your circumstances, or because you watched your dad react that way.

Now, if you think I am going to tell you to dismiss all your anger in your life and choose to be happy, then hold tight. Becoming angry is not a sin (see Ephesians 4:26). It can become a sin when the reason you get angry revolves around building you and your kingdom rather than promoting God's kingdom and the flourishing of others.

Men are known for getting angry, but what if men became known for being angry for righteous causes? Indeed, one *should* become angry when he witnesses something unjust. Biblical men, like Jesus, should show frustration at things that do not honor our heavenly father, his Word, or his church.[9]

If you're struggling with unrighteous anger, take time to evaluate what is at the root of the anger. Just as you can typically only see about 20 percent of an iceberg on the surface, in the same way you likely have about 80 percent of your reason for blowing up that has yet to be seen. Notice your triggers and make certain to process this with other people in your life.

- Is a particular wound, struggle, or frustration consistently beneath the surface of your anger that you need to work through?

- Do you get angry when your own pride or reputation is threatened?
- Have you asked the Lord to empower you to become angry at what he is angry at?

Animosity

Many of us are walking into our future while holding onto animosity, or unforgiveness, from the past. Maybe someone offended you, and you are still struggling to forgive them today. Maybe you are waiting for the other person to apologize, or you've convinced yourself that you have done nothing wrong.

Did someone say hurtful words to you years ago that you are still holding on to? Did someone do something that offended you? I'm willing to make the bet that at some point, every man holds on to unforgiveness in his heart.

The illusion of unforgiveness is that you are holding someone captive by your unforgiveness and that you are in control. You hold the offense over the other person as a baseball bat over their head. You think that the longer you draw it out, the more power you have over the other person. However, the other person is not the person being trapped; you are. Withholding forgiveness is, as Anne Lamott famously says, like you drinking rat poison and waiting for the rat to die. It doesn't work, and you'll continue to make yourself miserable until you choose to forgive.

What's important to remember is that forgiving someone else is not necessarily forgetting what happened in the past or minimizing the offense. Rather, it's acknowledging that the other person messed up and is sinful but choosing to look past the mistake and continue to love them.

Forgiveness is a one-way street, whereas reconciliation is two-way. You can forgive without the other person accepting or acknowledging it and without the restoration of your relationship. But forgiveness is always the first step in reconciliation and mending any broken relationships in your life.

You'll never be asked to forgive someone more than you've already been forgiven by Christ. It should be the overflow of your gratitude for Christ's mercy shown to you on the cross through his blood that ignites an act of forgiveness in your life. Even though forgiving someone might not make sense to you, it's what's required of you as a Christian (see Ephesians 4:32), and it's for your own good and for God's glory.

As you seek to forgive the offenses of your past, make forgiving others a part of your life continuously. People are imperfect, and offenses will come, so be ready to forgive others quickly. Be ready to, "Love your enemies, bless them that curse you, do good to them that hate you, and pray for them which despitefully use you, and persecute you" (Matt. 5:44 KJV). It's hard, but you'll be a better person because of it.

- Is there someone you are avoiding now that you need to forgive?
- How has unforgiveness caused bitterness in your own life?
- Who do you need to forgive now, but attempt to reconcile with later?

Anxiety

If you struggle with anxiety, please know that I have deep compassion for you and I hope that this is something that you are able to work through and find genuine freedom from. I want to encourage you to use your single season as a time to uncover the roots of your anxiety and to integrate new habits to help you heal in this area.

Mental Health expert Dr. John Delony says that anxiety is like an alarm telling you that there is a fire somewhere in the building.[10] Anxiety is typically a symptom of a deeper, potentially hidden, issue in your life. So, what might be anxiety trying to warn you about? Things like stress, loneliness, and family dynamics can contribute to anxiety.

As you notice anxiety in your life, it is important to process and heal intentionally. Men are more likely than women to "self-medicate" when it comes to anxiety. Don't try to get rid of your anxious feelings by drinking, gambling, working out more often, or over- or undereating. Instead, be sure you are spending a majority of your time in authentic and healthy Christian community and do not be afraid to share some of the challenges you are facing with someone else, especially a trusted pastor or counselor.

You might be anxious now, but perhaps this anxiety is trying to tell you something about how you're living your life and what needs to change. I encourage you: don't settle and make anxiety your identity. Be intentional, seek help, and pursue finding freedom in this area.

- Has anxiety become so frequent in my life that I have gotten used to it and ignored opportunities to find freedom from it?
- What challenges or stressors in my life could be contributing to me feeling anxious?
- What am I doing to actively seek growth in this area so that I do not find my identity in anxiety?

Alcohol

If you're a single guy in your mid-twenties, I'm not sure what other hobby is more popular than going to breweries around town. It seems like local craft beers, and maybe even some wine, too, are a prerequisite for a good social event these days.

God is concerned about the heart and motive behind what you drink. If your intention with drinking is to enjoy it in modest amounts, then your motive might be where it should be. But if you're drinking to feel approved by others or, worse yet, to get drunk, you need to examine your heart.

The Bible permits the consumption of alcohol while at the same time warning of its dangers. Alcohol consumption can be entertaining and a great way to meet new people. It can also manipulate people and fuel the fire of sin.

If you have struggled with alcohol abuse in the past or if your family has a history of alcohol abuse, you need to be extremely careful. In fact, if alcohol has frequently caused you to sin, you should consider whether it ought to have any place in your life at all.

For me, eliminating alcohol was the cost of following Christ. I didn't like who I was when I consumed alcohol, and I used it to numb my sense of conviction when I wanted to do something sinful. Because of this, just a few years ago, I decided to take a yearlong fast from alcohol. This one-year fast turned into three years, and it proved to be a powerful practice in my life.

Remember that God is allowing you to be single right now to do something in and through you. Chasing the appetite of alcohol is most likely not why God has you in the season of singleness right now.

• Is my enjoyment of alcohol continuously keeping me from investing my time in others?
• When I experience challenges or stressful situations, do I find myself turning to alcohol to help me?
• Could the money I spend on alcohol be redirected toward something of greater eternal value for God's kingdom?

Abuse

Throughout the last few years of discipling men and hearing the different stories and pain-points, I have noticed that indeed there are many men who have been abused sexually, physically, emotionally, or verbally in their past.

When it comes to sexual abuse, one in six males are abused in the United States before they turn eighteen. What's worse is that 90 percent of these men have been abused by someone they know or whom their family trusts. The majority of men who are abused do not admit to being sexually abused until later in life. Men often delay sharing about their abuse because they feel shame or fear what others might think. Often men don't share their abuse because they think that the abuse that happened wasn't actual abuse.[11]

Maybe you were abused in your past, but you haven't admitted it yet because you can't believe that it happened to you, and you feel shame about it. Or maybe you need to evaluate and dig deep and determine if the abuse that happened to you was indeed abuse. The odds are if you are thinking of an event in your life that happened and has been kept silent for years, it could be abuse that you need to work through.

Not addressing emotional, sexual, and physical abuse in your life can be dangerous for many reasons. Men who face abuse are prone to consequential hardships long-term. If you elect to conceal this abuse, you are ultimately wreaking havoc on yourself.

Furthermore, for many, abuse experienced in their past is the root cause of present struggles. That might be hard to hear. For example, men who were abused by other men often deal with perceived shame, rejection, and fear toward the other men in their lives. Abuse also has the power to distort your own attractions and channel them to the wrong place. Abuse that is left untouched and minimized often leads to depression, substance abuse, eating disorders, suicidal thoughts, lower academic performance, and increased promiscuity.

No matter who you are and what you struggle with, ask the Lord to reveal to you if you were abused physically, emotionally, or sexually in your life. Then, find a trusted friend, pastor, or counselor to work through this issue with so that you can begin to find healing. It's worth the time, energy, and money that you commit to it, and I am confident you'll be a better person as you allow this wound to heal over time.

- Has shame or embarrassment kept you from admitting an experience of abuse to someone else?
- Have you made an effort to forgive the man or woman who abused you in your past?
- How has the abuse in your past informed the way that you are living today and how you view yourself?

Attractions

Many men remain single because they are not attracted to women. If you struggle with being attracted to men, let me say: I'm sorry. You did not ask for these attractions, and no matter how badly you want to like a woman relationally, sexually, or emotionally, the desires you want never seem to come. The places and people that should be the most welcoming to you have likely brought about shame and forced you into isolation, prompting you to try to fix this issue on your own.

You are not alone. Many men have desires in conflict just like you do, and there is abundant freedom and healing to be discovered. I encourage you to be honest about this struggle with a godly peer who doesn't share this struggle, and with an older pastor or mentor. God does not waste anything, and he will use your past and your pains in this area for his good.

The ultimate goal of men who struggle with same-sex attraction should not be for them to become "heterosexual," but rather it should be for them to pursue holiness. God may or may not allow you to become attracted to the opposite sex, but their struggle should be for a holy lifestyle. Afterall, holiness should be the goal for those who do and do not struggle with this. Everyone should seek to be more conformed into the image of Christ the Son each day.

If you do not struggle with same-sex attraction, the chances are you know someone who does, or you will soon. I have had the opportunity to disciple many men who struggle with this, and it truly has been so rewarding. Being a present, available, and loving brother in Christ is the best thing you can do to help someone heal from this. Offering consistent love, encouragement, hope, grace, and truth is what everyone needs, no matter what they battle, and these men are no exception. You might be surprised at how similar the fight for purity is between men struggling with same-sex attraction and you.

- Have I made heterosexuality the goal rather than holiness?
- Am I allowing the experience of same-sex attraction to disqualify me from enjoying community with other men or disqualify me from marriage?
- How can I love and support other men who struggle with same-sex attraction?

Addictions

For years, I didn't think the word *addiction* applied to my life. I always thought people with addictions were the ones in the mental health facility or in prison somewhere. Little did I know that I was really being held prisoner by addictions in my own life.

Our brains and bodies become dependent on the things that we do consistently over time. There are a lot of things in our lives that are not bad things necessarily; an excess of a good thing can easily become a bad thing. The odds are, you might be addicted in your life to something that is good, but this thing might be holding you captive and holding the keys to your identity more than it should be. Checking your email can be a good thing but checking it too often and letting your messages (or lack thereof) affect your mood or worth can be a problem. Maybe you're reliant on caffeine, tobacco, or attention from others.

God doesn't mind us doing fun things over and over, he just doesn't want the things that we enjoy to own us. You need to ask yourself if the things you eat, watch, read, or drink are coming between you and your relationship with the Lord. God is a jealous God and he deeply longs to spend intimate time with you daily. He's allowed you to be single right now so that you may become concerned about his own heart.

For a season in my life, I used to fast from something different each month. I did this so that I could ensure I was not becoming dependent on or finding my value in something worldly. I've taken breaks from coffee, chewing gum, social media, and even traveling, to be sure I am locked in and focused on the God who created me and not a god that has been created in my life.

For some of you, you know exactly what addiction is keeping you hostage, but for others you need to spend some time thinking about what habit, substance, or even relationship you have become addicted to.

- Can I go one week without _____?
- Am I trying to keep _____ a secret?
- If I didn't do _____, would I still be confident in who I am?

Appearance

If I could be honest with you for a second, the struggle of appearance and body image has been the greatest wound of my life. Much of my single years account for me working out to achieve an ideal body type or chasing the right clothes to be accepted by other people. For years, I have been paralyzed with how others view my body. But by God's grace, many of my single years have also been filled with the Lord helping me to find freedom in this area.

This issue is often labeled as a female issue and talked about in women's contexts, but from my own experience as well as many other testimonies from men, I know that guys deeply struggle with body image as well. I'm sorry if this has been a struggle in your life.

What is interesting about this struggle is that it makes us do crazy things because we think that we can win over the approval of other people, but really, we just need the approval from ourselves. The hate that you have toward your body causes you to live in a prison of your own thoughts and the perceived thoughts of everyone else. Idolizing, abusing, punishing, or neglecting your physical body is a form of sin, as it does not honor the God-given temples that our bodies are.

I can remember people saying hurtful words to me about my physical body when I was younger. Maybe you can too. Maybe you find yourself looking in the mirror frequently and becoming disappointed or frustrated by what you see. Do you starve yourself from meals because you think you have too much body fat? Do you constantly look at other men to see how you measure up to them? Do you work out more than you should because if you just get that little bit of extra muscle then you think you'll be happy with your body?

How you find freedom in this area of your life will be unique from how anyone else will. It might look like starting to forgive the people who said hurtful things about your body when you were younger. It might look like finding and praying verses that tell the truth about your body (for example, 1 Samuel 16:7 or Philippians 3:20–21). It might mean opening up to a brother in Christ and being brutally honest about your approach to your own body.

In one season, I spent an entire year praying each morning and night for my physical body. While on my knees praying, I would put my hands on my body and ask God to help me see my body how he sees it and for me to stop idolizing and abusing my body. I saw immense amounts of fruit in my life from doing this.

You cannot afford to continue living your life like this. The self-love or self-hate toward your own body is deadly and will affect your circles of influence if you do not address this now. God has given you this time of singleness to uproot some of these dangerously toxic mindsets that you have toward yourself.

- What habits do you do with the hope of winning other people's approval of your physical appearance?
- What would it look like to honor your physical body?
- How might this issue become a worse issue if you do not take time to address it now?

Chapter 11

Heart over Habits

There is a direct correlation between your relationship with God and the progress you make in your life toward freedom from your sin. It would be ignorant and unwise for a Christian man to attempt to fix his sins and bad habits with more discipline in his life. Though discipline is very useful (and we will talk about that soon), your commitment to and relationship with God ultimately has the power to transform your life.

Imagine a married couple who is faithfully committed to one another. When there is faithfulness from both spouses, the idea of cheating on each other seems far-fetched and likely isn't even desired. When the two are intimate, committed, and display deep affection for each other, the inclination to sin is decreased. In the same way, as your level of intimacy with the Lord increases, your inclination to sin will decrease. Your relationship with the Lord is the most important area of your life to develop and grow while you are single.

Human beings are designed to be intimate with God. Before sin entered the world, man was in perfect communion with God. Satan, the great tempter, convinced Adam and Eve that they didn't need to trust God and instead could trust the ways of the world. This is the same temptation you face each day.

Many people think Satan exists to tempt you to do bad things, and he does. But more often than not, Satan will tempt you to change your perspective on God. Satan wants to convince you that God isn't all you need. He wants to tell you that there is something else in this world that will offer more gratification and satisfaction than the pleasures of God himself. Satan is liar.

Each day you are faced with a choice. The two decisions that loom before you are: do you trust that God's way is better, or do you want to trust in your own discernment and judgments?

When you sin, the pride in your life tells you that your way is better than God's way. When the pride grows, sin takes full root and devours the small intentions of doing good you have in your life. Therefore, in order to find freedom in your life, you need to understand and operate from the identity that Jesus Christ awarded you. When you are one with him, the lures of temptation might not go away, but they will seem less appealing, and you will be more likely to intentionally draw upon the Lord to help you through your temptations.

Your ability to defeat and get past the temptation in your life is based more on your relationship with God than it is on self-control. Let that sink in. I'm willing to bet that for years you've tried to stop sinning by only attacking sin. You have told yourself no to countless temptations, yet you've indulged in more porn, masturbation, sex, and lust than you care to admit. These things are symptoms of a greater issue deep down. These acts reveal a misplaced identity and a decision to operate outside of God's identity for you. Sin within the human race has thwarted a consistent and perfect relationship with the Father. Most people try to fix the issue by fixing the symptoms. If all you focus on are the symptoms without fixing the issue beneath the surface, you'll be running in place your whole life.

I believe that as you shift your approach toward God, you'll become more likely to follow him and to trust him. Only God can help you break free from some of the darkest thoughts and sins plaguing your life.

I also believe that as you grow in your relationship with God, you'll be able to hear from him more as well. During my mid-twenties I realized I had some anger at God because I wasn't hearing his voice clearly and I wasn't able to understand his will. But soon God revealed to me that it wasn't his voice that was small, but it was my own actions of consistent disobedience that were fueling pride and making me blind and deaf to what God was saying to me. As you rake back some of the impurities in your life and begin to enjoy a relationship with God, your ability to hear from him will increase.

As we think about ordering our lives in a way that is pleasing and glorifying to God, we need to keep a few things in mind:

Obedience Flows from a Love for God

In the first part of this book, we uncovered what your identity in Jesus is. You are a son of God. You are a temple of the Holy Spirit and an instrument for God's purpose. The byproducts of abiding in the truth of God should be obedience and right living. On the flip side, when you decide to place your identity in something that is not of God, pride and sin will be the byproducts.

Your aim in singleness should be to fall in love with God so much that disobeying him feels farfetched. When you are intimate with God, being disobedient should feel like betrayal to him.

Furthermore, as you fall deeper in love with him, you should grow in joy to honor and obey what God commands of you. As a husband loves his wife and seeks to honor her through his service, words, and actions, so should you and I seek to honor God because of our love for him.

Obedience is More Liberating Than Binding

Freedom is not something that most people associate with rules and following orders, but the truth is, the law, the rules, the commandments in Scripture, and the instructions from Jesus himself do not exist merely to suppress you or to minimize what you can do. Instead they serve for your good, and they actually give you more freedom in the long run.

Think about a stop light. What do you do when the light is red? You stop. You obey the law that has been set in place because it leads to human flourishing overall. Imagine if no one acknowledged the stop light and instead decided to go when it was red. You'd quickly have chaos, and it would be dangerous to you and everyone else. You wouldn't have the freedoms in life you're used to if you're constantly in car accidents at the stop light.

What you can learn for your own life is that God's will, expressed in his commands, promotes freedom, not oppression. God, who knows what is best for you, has established rules as guidelines for you to live a free life, a life within his ultimate blessing and with your good in mind. And guess what? There is grace available for you every single time when you miss the mark.

Obedience Affects More Than Yourself

In college, I decided to try a new sport, so I joined the rowing team. In rowing, every teammate in the boat must do his job in sync with the other team members so that the boat can be propelled forward as fast as possible. If you miss your cue and place your oar in the water too soon or too late, you will cause the boat to slow down or shift directions. The actions of each person in the boat affects everyone else.

Your obedience and disobedience always affect someone else. Whether you realize it or not, anytime you choose to be disobedient you always affect more people than just yourself. Obedience can do great damage. Lust turns daughters of God into sex objects and distorts the way you view, interact, and learn from women. Masturbation fogs the mind and dissolves your motivation to serve others wholeheartedly. Watching porn sets unrealistic standards for your future wife and leads you to disappointments with your spouse down the road. Sin always affects someone else even if you don't notice it right away.

Think about it this way: your sin has never blessed anyone. And even if there is a sin that you think is just in the dark and kept secret, it has and will have an effect on others. God is always watching and reminds us that he "will bring every deed into judgement, including every hidden thing, whether it is good or evil" (Ecc. 12:14 NIV).

For me, I found that the times in the day I chose to look at pornography were early in the morning or late in the evenings, both times I should have been spending with the Lord (see Psalm 1). I just think about how much deeper my relationship with the Lord could be right now if I had spent the hundreds of hours I spent on porn and worldly things on my relationship with God instead. When I lived life in perpetual sin, I noticed how damaged my relationships with others—both men and women—

became. I was shorter with people, I had less joy to offer friends, and I wasn't thinking of how to serve or encourage the people closest to me. Sin penetrates deep. No one has ever been blessed by your disobedience, and everyone in your life needs you to be obedient.

Being obedient to the commands God has laid out in his Word might be frustrating to you, confusing, difficult, or plain-out annoying. But remember that as a son of God, you are called to conduct yourself in a way that reflects your heavenly Father. God, through his Spirit, is always available, no matter where you are or what time of the day it is, to help you and give you the power to change.

A Question
Do you believe that God's commandments exist for your own good?

A Single Shift
Read 1 John 5:2-3 and meditate on this passage.

A Prayer
Lord, thank you for the life that you have given me. God, you know that I am on a journey to find freedom from some of my darkest and most consistent sins. God, as I understand that my sin dishonors you, would you help me to draw closer to you each day so that the temptations of sin would become less appealing? God help me to prioritize you over any habits or disciplines that I set. Thank you for helping me with the sin in my life. Amen.

Chapter 12

How Habits Help

Ultimately, you can try to install a million habits in your life to prevent yourself from being sexually impure or giving into sin, but if you do not have love for God and a blossoming relationship with him, you will struggle to find freedom in your life.

At the same time, as you walk with God, the right habits will be extremely useful in your journey toward freedom. Living in a world with temptation on every corner, honoring obedience to God's Word rarely makes sense to us. The pressures of modern culture and the actions of our friends will try to tell us that compromising on obedience is okay and that it can be good for us. By installing good habits and disciplines in your life, you can overcome the temptations of the moment and override the deep desires that you face.

We must set these habits with an awareness that you won't want to do them when the time comes. See, it's easy to talk about good habits and disciplines that you should put in your life, but these habits are only useful if they are put into action. Habits are not only about doing the right things, but also doing the right things at the right times.

Additionally, we should keep in mind that freedom can be found through a combination of small habits. Craig Groechel says, "Sometimes, the smallest acts of obedience and trust lead to the biggest results, the biggest blessings, and the biggest miracles."[12] Your acts of obedience have the potential to have residual benefits over a lifetime. The best approach you can have is to be obedient in the small decisions you have right in front of you; that's all you are called to do right now. It is through these small shifts in your single years that you will find the freedom you desire.

I know you want to break free from the struggles that are holding you back, so I encourage you to learn from the one who was sinless on earth. Study the life of Jesus, spend time alone with him, and pray with him often and begin to implement the habits that he implemented in his life. Read what he has already said to you through his Word and meditate on his truth daily. Your desire to sin will decrease when your intimacy with him increases.

The habits I encourage you to focus on and build are the ones that can be implemented and put into action when you face your greatest temptations. Even as I get closer to God, I still experience an overwhelming number of temptations each day. In fact, as I have grown closer to the Lord and lived on purpose for the kingdom more and more, my temptations have gotten much worse. I am constantly faced with new opportunities and spaces to indulge into my own desires of the flesh. I cannot act surprised or even frustrated when I face these temptations. Having temptations is going to be a part of my life as long as I am on this side of heaven, so it is critical that I establish ways in which I can turn, run, and flee from these temptations.

I have to constantly reframe the temptations in my life. These temptations remind me that I desire something rich, relational, and rewarding. The truth is, I can fulfill these desires through time with God.

Pay attention to the temptations in your life. Satan cannot create anything; thus he often uses the same tactics to try to get you to fall into sin and distrust God.

Now, when I get the urge to look at porn, I channel these desires into time in prayer. When I have these urges, I will often go for a walk, call a friend, work out, or do something else to get my mind off the temptation I feel.

When it comes to my technology, for years I did not sleep with my phone in my room because I did not want the temptation of looking at porn to be just a few feet away from me. (Plus, when your alarm clock goes off on your phone in another room, it forces you to get up out of bed to turn it off!) Having a filtering software like Covenant Eyes on all my devices has been extremely helpful to me. Every time I search something on any of my devices, I have someone looking over my shoulder. I do not have access to the App Store on any of my devices. If I want to download an app, I must ask my accountability partner to enter a code and download the app for me.

A few years ago, I noticed that I was most tempted to look at porn after getting home from church, an event, or a trip. So now, every time I return to my empty house, I get on my knees and pray, asking the Lord to spare me from temptations and give me his strength to choose light over darkness.

When I face the temptation to lust, I shift my eyes to my purpose and the work God has laid out before me. If you know that you lust often at the gym or another place, text a brother to pray for you as you enter these locations. Sometimes when I am very tired and I know that I am more prone to lust, I will avoid going to the gym or to places where I know I will likely give in to lustful thoughts.

There have been seasons in my life when my accountability partner and I would send a check mark emoji to each other each night if we went through the day without giving into porn or masturbation. Truthfully, we don't even go through a day without sinning, and our love from God is not contingent on getting a green check mark, but this system did help both of us in the seasons of life we were in.

With the right mindset, our temptations bring us closer to God and remind us of our utter dependence on him as a protector and provider. God will always take what Satan intends for evil, and he will use it for his own good. The temptations you face every day have the unbelievable power to draw you closer to your heavenly Father.

Don't get mad at yourself when you face temptations. Everyone faces temptations—even Jesus. You will see attractive people, and you will be alone on your computer at night. But instead of indulging, shift these desires into sweet and rich time with God.

When I fail, I have to remind myself that God is infinitely kind to me and that he wants to continue a relationship with me despite my shortcomings. I confess and repent to God immediately after I sin, even if it's hard, because I know it's in those moments he wants to show me his perfect love and strength. I have been humbled that God has used some of my worst mistakes and transformed them into some of my greatest lessons. Nothing is ever wasted in God's world, and he will use your past to build a stronger man in your future.

Up to this point, we have worked through what it means and looks like for you to uncover your identity. As you have discovered this and begun to live within these truths, we moved into one of the greatest uses of your season of singleness, which is finding freedom. I hope that areas of your life that have been kept in the dark have been illuminated and that you feel inspired and empowered to move past some of your deepest sins and struggles. As you do that, you clear the way for the fun part of singleness. Once you uncover your identity and find freedom, you are now ready to go all-in on some of the greatest opportunities that singleness affords you. I want to give you ten opportunities that I think you can (and should) take advantage of as a single guy.

A Question

What boundaries do you have with your technology to prevent you from giving into sin online and what kind of accountability do you have?

A Single Shift

Consider the times you get tempted the most. Find a new habit to begin during these moments that will help you cultivate a deeper relationship with God.

A Prayer

God, thank you for loving me so much to choose me as a son. Lord, help me to recognize the times, places, and events that cause me to be tempted. Would you teach me to use these temptations as moments to honor you? Continue to show me how my sin affects others and myself and empower me to build wise and effective habits and boundaries in my life to cultivate a righteous life. I love you, Lord. Amen.

PART THREE
Notice Opportunities

Chapter 13

Establish Habitual Servanthood

Singleness is no doubt a blessing and a season of life that God has called many men to. As we consider the hundreds of opportunities that singleness does afford, I want to tell you about one, if not the greatest, opportunity that singleness affords you right now. This opportunity is often neglected by guys, but I think this is something that will really bless you in your life.

God has designed marriage in such a way that it is ultimately a sacrifice. Both partners enter a covenant together to promote and uphold the well-being of each other, sacrificing the priority of their own desires. As you are possibly called to a life of marriage one day, it is important to be thinking about the demands of marriage and how you can be preparing for it while you are single.

Seeking the good of another requires dying to yourself. Many times it requires surrendering to your own desires and preferences and allowing the other person to flourish even if it's hard for you. You could ask almost any married couple, and they'd quickly tell you that they can't always have their own way. Instead, much of their relationship is them figuring out how they can sacrificially love one another.

Everyone, not just those who are married, should constantly be in a posture of serving others by sacrificing their own time, energy, money, and resources. When you're married, you are permanently attached to the opportunity of sacrifice, and each day you are given the opportunity (or face the obligation) to give yourself away. Men who are single are not faced with this daily obligation, and it can be easy to become focused on one's own self. It is crucial that singles actively seek to find ways to sacrificially give themselves away through service to others.

During my first semester in seminary, I had a period of feeling extremely discontent, ungrateful, and anxious in my mind. I was driving myself crazy, stressing myself out over the clothes I was wearing, worried to death over other people's thoughts of me, and having trouble focusing in class because I was consumed with thoughts about myself. It seemed like the more I was thinking about myself, the worse off I was, and in every thought and in every moment, I was becoming more and more miserable.

I had become so frustrated with being consumed with myself that I decided that I needed to shift the focus off myself and on to someone else. After class, I went to McDonald's and picked up fifteen hamburgers. I decided I was going to pass them out to some homeless people downtown. I was in desperate need to shift my attention from myself to others, and this was the only thing I could think of to do. I parked my car near where I had noticed homeless people before, hugged a big brown bag of McDonald's burgers in my arms, and began to walk around town.

It wasn't long until I found plenty of men and women to give the burgers to. As I gave one burger out, others quickly flocked toward me, and it was clear that I was going to need more burgers. When I handed these homeless men and women a burger, it was as if I had handed them a million dollars; they were so grateful, and it was incredible to see smiles fill their faces. Gratefully, I had some great conversations with Vanessa, Lisa, and a man who went by the name "Duck." I had the opportunity to pray with several of these men and women and shared my own faith with them too.

There is a mysterious equation when it comes to serving. Serving seems like it would be something that will drain you, your bank account, and your time, but in God's economy, serving will always leave you more lifted up then when you started. You might be more tired, hungrier, and have less money than before you started, but you'll feel more fulfilled, content, and satisfied, and you can go to sleep that night knowing that God used you to add value to someone.

Your life is rigged to require serving, but it's up to you to initiate it. You must dictate when you serve and how you do it, so it is crucial for single guys to intentionally create, plan, and execute means in which they can serve.

One of the best opportunities you have right now in your single years is to establish habitual servanthood. Serving is going to be a necessity for the rest of your life, and you are in a unique place right now to begin to establish this crucial habit so that it may last a lifetime. Just as one would go on a mission trip to serve for a week or a month, you have an incredible opportunity right now to establish your single years as a mission trip that is continuously unfolding.

If you do happen to get married one day, you'll be serving your wife and family all the time, but you'll also want to find ways to serve your community. If it's hard for you to establish servanthood in your single years, then think about how challenging it will be to initiate serving others once you're much busier later in life.

When I think about serving during my single years, I love to get creative. After all, I don't have a wife I need to run my plans by and there are a lot of things I can do that no one really ever needs to know about. Once you begin to get creative in how you can serve others, you won't be able to stop, and you'll be brainstorming all kinds of ways you can sacrifice yourself for the flourishing of others.

Right now, I like to think about serving in three different spheres: time, talents, and resources. I've listed a few ideas in which you can begin to serve in each of these areas right now:

Time
- Text a Bible verse or encouragement to a friend.
- Pray for your friends and ask for prayer requests from them.
- Help your roommates with household chores.
- Listen intentionally in a conversation.
- Give compliments to someone.
- Pick up garbage in your neighborhood.

Talents
- Get involved on a team at your church.
- Become a mentor for a high school or middle school student.
- Find a local organization to give your time to.
- Provide a service for someone for free liking mowing lawn or washing a car.

Resources
- Donate household items to a local donation center.
- Surprise a co-worker with a coffee.
- Invite someone over for dinner.
- Sponsor a child overseas.[13]
- Buy and mail a book to someone.
- Text a digital gift card to someone.

I hope you are beginning to see how creative serving can be and how much freedom you have to customize and tailor how you serve others.

One thing you should keep in mind is that you should aim to serve others through the means of your own gifting. You know you have specific spiritual gifts and natural abilities that are unique to you, and as you seek to serve others it is best to operate out of those strengths. As you seek out new opportunities to serve more often, you'll be able to truly serve someone best when you are operating from the strengths you have. If you avoid using your giftings as a way to serve others, you rob both the people you are serving and the body of Christ. The world needs you to be you and use the strengths that God has placed within you.[14]

It's funny to me how many times we pray for God to make us more content, satisfied, and joyful with our lives when he has already given us the tools to do so. Activating the strengths we have within us for the purpose of someone else's good is one of the quickest ways to find fulfillment and contentment.

When you put yourself in a place around others who are working and serving with similar giftings that you have, you never know what sorts of connections you might make with people along the way. The people you serve with might offer you a job or connect you to someone helpful down the road. One time I decided to talk to and encourage the lady next to me on a plane, and she unexpectedly ended up giving me $250 to put toward my mission trip! You never know how serving might bless you in return. Of course, this should never be the motive behind serving, and instead, we should seek to serve out of our love for God and people.

As you seek to find new ways to serve others, bring some friends along and journey into this exciting adventure together. Some of your greatest life experiences are on the other side of your obedience to serve others. Many underestimate the power of what serving can do. It can change lives, shape cultures, give us fulfillment, and impact the trajectory of your future. I'm curious how long it will take you before you begin to see the power that comes through serving!

Since these ten chapters are full of practical steps and shifts for you to take right now, you won't find a specific "single shift" at the end of each chapter. Instead, I'll provide some questions and a suggested prayer as you consider how to put each opportunity into action.

A Question
Who in my life has God already placed in front of me to serve?

A Prayer
Lord, thank you for giving me a body that is able to serve others. Please help me to prioritize helping, serving, and loving others during my single season. Show me the places you are calling me to serve and help cultivate a joy-filled, servant-heart among me. Amen.

Chapter 14

Cultivate Abiding in Christ

"Are you still watching?" This is the phrase we see on our TV screens when we've been binge watching a TV show and Netflix thinks we've fallen asleep. Silly Netflix.

Now there is certainly nothing wrong with watching Netflix, but I find it interesting that one of the biggest complaints that I hear from guys is that they are not growing in their relationship with the Lord and that they feel like they have "hit a wall" in their spiritual growth. And at the same time, I see so many of these guys who have this desire to go deeper in their faith spend so much of their time on fruitless activities.

So many people want to see the fruit of a disciplined Christian life without having to do the work. But to live a life as a Christian whose growth in God, whose sanctification, is constantly growing, we must integrate habits and disciplines in life that can help you get there.

First Timothy tells us, "Train yourself to be godly… [because] godliness has value for all things, holding promise for both the present life and the life to come" (1 Tim. 4:7-8 NIV). We as Christians are called to train ourselves so that we promote a more holy and godly life. The greatest thing you can pursue in your life right now is the discipline to become more holy. This is why singleness exists. To pursue what absolutely matters most, you pursue becoming a better version of yourself, a version that is more identical to the person of Jesus Christ and who is less identical to the patterns of the world. Becoming more godly is the best way to make use of the time you have while you are single, and I believe that God grants and allows singleness in many guys' lives so that they may become more holy and purified as men of God.

This is why you are single. You are single to pursue to what matters most: to pursue holiness and to clothe yourself with person of Jesus Christ every single day.

But how do you do that? The odds are you have tried to live a more holy life in the past. Maybe you heard it from your pastor in college or a trusted friend from your small group encouraged you to pursue godliness and take your faith more seriously. As you strive to do, you'll need a plan or some actionable steps that you can take to invest in your spiritual growth. If you don't have a plan to get to your destination, you'll remain stuck where you are starting.

Pursuing what matters most begins with discipline. Spiritual disciplines are the stepping stones to a more holy version of yourself.

For the last nine years in my life, I have tried to consistently integrate several spiritual disciplines in order to become more like Christ. Here are seven disciplines you can start integrating in your life this week to grow your relationship with the Lord.

Meditate on Scripture

When I was three years old, my parents taught my siblings and me Psalm One, and we spent time around the dinner table memorizing this passage and rehearsing the chapter with hand motions. One of the lines that has stuck out to me the most now that I'm a man in my mid-twenties is "blessed is the one…who meditates on his law day and night" (v. 1-2 NIV). I have always thought it interesting how the Bible uses the word "meditate" instead of "read." I have found that there is a great difference between reading God's word and meditating on it.

Many people read God's Word. Some read it daily, weekly, or perhaps monthly, but if you were to ask them what they read just a few hours after reading it, it is likely they will have no recollection of it. Indeed, even non-Christians or atheists read God's Word. However, to meditate on God's Word is to receive everything God has stored within his Word and then apply it to one's life.

Stay with me here, but we've all seen cows grazing out in a pasture, eating grass. When a cow eats, it swallows the food and some of the food is moved into its stomach. However, much of the food, once swallowed, will be sent back towards their mouth into the rumen where a cow will work to process all the needed nutrients from the food. Once a cow absorbs the nutrients, the food is then passed down to the stomach. This process is known as "chewing the cud" and throughout the day the cow will continue to ruminate over the food that they have taken in.

Like the cow (sorry, no offense!), you should continue to chew throughout the day on the truths you take in from Scripture. God told Joshua that if he were to meditate on his Word day and night then he would be "prosperous and successful" (Josh. 1:8 NIV). Meditating on God's Word is how you will become closer to looking like Christ and as a single guy, you should have the time to do this consistently in your life.

Solitude

When I found out I was going to be spending five hours by myself in solitude one afternoon on a retreat I attended my freshman year, I was terrified. *What if I get bored?* I thought. *What if I fall asleep and can't get back to camp once it's dark?* These were all excuses I wanted to make to spend that time with my friends instead, but truthfully I was more scared to be alone by myself with God.

The Bible tells us over and over about how much time Jesus spent in solitary places. Luke tells us that "Jesus often withdrew to lonely places and prayed" (5:16 NIV). Being alone with God reconnects us to our Father, who is deeply in love with us, and it realigns our priorities to his. Like a date between a man and woman, time with God exists to grow intimacy, deepen connection, and increase understanding.

I always think it's funny how so many guys complain about a lack of clarity from God or being unable to discern his will, but when I ask them if they have spent extended time alone with him the answer proves the reason. I credit some of my greatest lessons in life to time spent in solitude with the Lord. I was jogging on a beach when God revealed to me my calling in life. I was at a state park in Indiana when I uncovered the

Lord's will for my business and ministry. Time alone in the countryside of Germany is where God began to show me what he was going to do with some of my pains and sufferings in life. I encourage you to try to spend an extended amount of time with God once a week and during this time implement these spiritual disciplines.

Finding time to be alone with God will be more challenging to do once you're married. As a single man, make it a priority to spend time alone with the Lord now, so that if you do get married, you will work to continue the momentum of this habit.

Worship

Worshipping God is something that you were created to do. We are designed, empowered, and expected to worship God continually, not just at Sunday morning church services.

Every single person on earth worships something, but not everyone worships God. As a human in a sinful world, you will have to consistently fight a battle to align your body to worship the true king.

One great way to bring God the praise and honor he desires from you is to sing songs of praise to him. My favorite worship songs are the ones that talk about God's person, his character, his holiness, his greatness, and his wonder. I will sometimes sing these songs to God in the mornings, driving to work or school, and in the evenings as I prepare to go to bed.

Disciplining yourself to spend time in worship will remind you of who you should worship and will protect your heart from worshipping something worldly. This will align your priorities throughout the day, and when challenges arise you can be reminded that a faithful God is in control. Create a set list of your favorite worship songs on your phone and spend time singing songs of praise each week.

You might have lots of time alone in the car or in your room at night. I encourage you during these times to make it a point to worship. As an unmarried man, you have abundant opportunities to worship and praise God throughout your day. Enjoy these times alone by worshipping the God who created you!

Confession

Pride naturally creeps in and attempts to convince us that we are perfect and without sin. But the reality is, all of us have fallen short of the glory of God and there is no one righteous among us (Rom. 3:23 CEV; Rom. 3:10 NIV).

I have found that spending a few minutes in confession each week reminds me of how broken I am and how desperate I am for a Savior. I try to spend time in confession both independently with God as well as with another brother in Christ.

Telling God the sins I have committed in the past six days helps me to see the gospel of Jesus Christ in a more rich way as he reminds me that his death and resurrection have covered the punishment of my sins. Sometimes I will journal my sins and list them out just so I can see what Christ has paid for me. Other times, I will speak out loud to God the sins that I have committed.

As I confess my sins to other brothers, I am kept accountable in the future as I am less likely to sin when I know that another brother is watching and that I will need to confess my sins to him later. Confession has the ability to strengthen any relationship or organization that you are part of. Becoming comfortable with confessing with someone now will enable you to apologize and confess more freely as a husband, which is great leadership for the whole house to witness. Confession creates peace when done willingly and when forgiveness is sought and will surely propel your walk as a disciple of Christ.

Celebration

If you're anything like me, when you reach the end of your to-do list, there seems to magically appear more tasks to get done and slave away at. The reality is, there is always something else to do, so taking time to pause and celebrate is essential.

By taking time to celebrate, you can be reminded of how God is using you and you can be enlightened to how God's faithfulness allowed you to carry out certain tasks in your life. I like to treat myself to certain meals or desserts when I reach a milestone in my life. Being single, it can become easy to overlook this disciple and not take the time to celebrate what God has done in your life. Be sure to share your wins with others and invite them to celebrate with you.

Writing

We all know that thinking about personal growth or processing our past is a helpful thing to do. But sometimes, we need to do more than just think about what is going on in our lives. Writing down your thoughts, experiences, and prayers is a great way to thoroughly process what God is doing in you, remain distraction free, and to be more intentional about understanding the season of life you are in. As a single guy, you should spend time writing out confessions, celebrations, concerns, and conversations with God.

You never know how these writing might serve you well in the future and could serve as a powerful reminder to you of the Lord's faithfulness in your life. Who knows, maybe your prayers and journals will become a way to encourage someone through a book one day. (I might know this from experience!).

Rest Well

When we have a day off or a break from school, it can be tempting to fill our time with entertainment. But resting well sometimes means intentionally spending your down time to grow your relationship with the Lord. You need rest, and Scripture encourages us to rest weekly in the same way that God rested from his work of Creation.

I have found that I am more energized and productive during a week when I make rest before the week starts a priority. Rather than working *toward* rest, I have found it better to work *from* rest. Take time each week to rest fully, spending that time in a way that brings life to you and enrichment to your relationship with the Lord.

Neglecting to intentionally integrate rest in your life now will surely have its consequences but imagine neglecting to do this when life gets even busier down the road. Take the time now to build the muscle of implementing a day of rest in your weekly routine so that you may be fully available and ready to what God calls you to do.

These practices you adopt won't just be useful to you now; they are truly disciplines that you will bring into the next seasons of your life, whatever they might be. If you aren't doing them now while you most likely have the most time in your life, it's unlikely you will adopt this habit into your life in the future when you're busier.

The first time in your life you try something new, the odds are you weren't likely very good at it. But by consistently working at your new hobby through practice, research, training and coaching, you are able to become more proficient or even professional at your habit. Have patience with yourself as you implement spiritual disciplines, but also take small steps one at a time to work towards becoming more godly.

Furthermore, when you think about the first time that you did a bicep curl, you might have found yourself using lighter weights since you aren't strong enough for the heavier stuff. But you don't want to spend your entire life using 20-pound dumbbells. Instead, you want to move up in weight over time. In the same way, as you grow spiritually, make sure your spiritual disciplines are growing too. Maybe you used to only spend ten minutes alone with God each day; how can you take this to the next level and instead spend thirty or sixty minutes with God?

These disciplines will bring you steps closer to God. The person God wants you to be, a disciple of Christ who spends time with him and learning from him to become more like him, starts with these disciplines on a daily basis. Paul tells us in Hebrews, "No discipline seems pleasant at the time, but painful. Later on, however, it produces a harvest of righteousness and peace for those who have been trained by it" (12:11 NIV). If you do not *feel* like integrating the disciplines in your life, I encourage you to press on and trust that the end result will be worth it.

A Question

If someone were to follow you around for one day, what evidence would there be in your life that you are a Christian seeking to grow in his faith?

A Prayer

Lord, thank you that I have the ability to grow in my faith rather than just stay stagnant. Would you please convict me of how I can better use the time that you have given me to grow in my relationship with you? Give me the motivation and intentionality I need to implement helpful disciplines in my life. Amen.

Chapter 15

Discover Financial Freedom

I'll never forget the day when I opened my banking app while in college and discovered that all the money to my name summed up to be a whopping $0.00. Then I checked my savings account and discovered another whopping $0.00. Fast forward a few years later, and after beginning a full-time salary position at a large company, I was getting some pretty decent paychecks deposited into my account. No matter which end of the spectrum you find yourself on right now, managing your finances well is something you must learn to do.

Money is extremely powerful. It has the power to build great things or the power to destroy and divide families. How you spend, invest, save, and give money should not be taken lightly. Jesus knew the significance of money, and of his thirty-eight parables we have recorded in the Bible, sixteen were on the topic of money and possessions. Furthermore, while there are more than five hundred verses about prayer and faith in scripture, there are two thousand verses concerning money and possessions.

What you do with your money matters, and though it may seem like you are only affecting yourself with your cash, you're not. You have a unique opportunity now during your single years to not only practice wise and biblical financial principles but also to set yourself up for a life of faithful stewardship.

Money is a useful tool because money reveals the motives of our hearts. Jesus tells us this in Matthew 6:21 when he says, "For where your treasure is, there your heart will be also" (NIV). Our spending habits, saving habits, and investing habits all reveal something deeper about ourselves than what is on the surface. Money magnifies the motives and priorities within our hearts.

The truth is you don't own anything that you think you own. Your money, house, car, body—you name it—is not yours, but rather God's. God has chosen to gift you these things and to make you a manager of his assets. The question becomes how good of a manager do you want to be for your heavenly Father who has entrusted these things to you? Let's talk about some of the ways you can work toward being a good manager of the money that God has given you.

Give

It surprises me that many single guys, especially those with full-time salaries, neglect the habit of giving. Jesus calls us to give our money and by neglecting to do so we disobey him. As a Christian, you should strive to give a portion of your income always, no matter what season of life you are in.

Some of the happiest and most content people I know are the most generous people I know. Think about it, have you ever met an unhappy, generous person before? Generosity does something to you.

Ultimately, giving away money allows you to tell your money that it does not have control of you, but rather you have control over it. Giving gives you freedom over the temptation to hoard money and reminds you that God can do something through you to bless someone else through your generosity,

I love being creative in the way that I give. In fact, thinking of unexpected ways to bless others is the most fun I have with money. Each month, I go to my bank and ask for $100 in ten-dollar bills. Then, I challenge myself to give out each of those bills to people I come across in the grocery store, airport, or anywhere else. I also have a fund called the "Above and Beyond" fund, in which I set cash aside to give above what is required of me so that others may go beyond their potential. I have found that giving money away is the most fun you can have with it, and it will instill a sense of satisfaction and joy within you.

Debt

You don't have to look far to notice financial crises among all generations in America. According to the New York Fed, the four most common debts among millennials are student loans (taking up the majority), home mortgages, credit cards, and car loans.[15] According to data collected from one thousand millennials in 2016, the average millennial debt load is sitting right at $30,580, and many think they will die before their debt is paid in full.[16] Zooming out, 78 percent of Americans are living paycheck to paycheck[17] and 47 percent of Americans have less than $1,000 saved up for emergencies.[18]

Having debt is like having a cinder block around your neck; it prevents you from moving forward, keeping you stuck doing the same thing over and over again just to make ends meet. Debt is proven to be a reason for stress, anxiety, and worry, and it greatly limits your ability to invest and save for your future.

It is unfortunate how common financial debt has become in our culture. So many millennials and Gen Zers demand to have the standard of living right now that it took their parents their whole career to provide. The world will tell us that going into debt is the only way to get the things we need and want, and that staying in debt is a lifelong habit you need to get used to. Romans 13:8 tells us "Let no debt remain outstanding, except the continuing debt to love one another" (NIV). Avoiding debt by living on less than what you make will help you learn some of the best lessons of your life.

In the largest study ever conducted in North America on millionaires, researchers found that the number one key to becoming wealthy was staying out of debt and living on less than what you make.[19] It turns out, there are no shortcuts to becoming wealthy, and just like getting in shape with your body, becoming financially successful requires planning, diligence, patience, and work.

Budget

Many people hate the word *budget*, but a budget gives you more freedom than it does restrictions. Think of a budget as "permission to spend." Great things can happen when you have great planning. A budget is your way of you telling your money each month what it is going to do. You are in control of the money you make, invest, save, and spend, and you need to tell your money where to go.

Just like anything else in life, if you have a goal you want to hit you will need a plan to get from A to B. A budget is the written plan that puts you in control of your money. Find a budgeting app[20] or go old school and write out a monthly budget on a legal pad. However, you do it, you cannot win with money if you do not win with a budget.

Whether you are single for the rest of your life or if you will have a wife and children soon, you are responsible for the financial well-being of your family. First Timothy 5:8 tells us, "But if anyone does not provide for his relatives, and especially for members of his household, he has denied the faith and is worse than an unbeliever" (ESV). It is hard to provide for your family when you feel like money has its control on you. Providing for your family and your future generations starts right now with how you manage your finances.

Now, if you are like most men I talk to on a regular basis, you probably have your own way of handling your finances. You might agree with one of my points above but disagree on another. When it comes down to it, you are responsible for your own finances. Let me warn you, as a young man who is new to the finance world myself, that you don't know everything. I just don't know everything that goes into finances, which is why I have adapted my financial principles from the Bible and from other older and wiser men who have proven to win with money. Often a young man's own pride leads him to make the biggest mistake of his life, and this happens a lot with finances.

Take some time to work through your plan for managing your finances. Sit down with the quiet and humble financially stable people at your church and learn from them. Don't learn money principles from your broke friends. Best-selling author and financial coach Dave Ramsey has led millions of people out of debt and into a more sustainable and prosperous lifestyle, and through his afternoon radio talk show and books, I have learned from Dave many wise biblical financial principles. I would encourage you to check out his resources.[21]

The money and resources that you have now and will have in your future are not yours. In reality, everything is God's and God has been kind enough to entrust you as the manager to steward those resources. Will you slow down enough in your single season now to ensure you are being faithful to what God has given you?

A Question
What does the way you spend your money reveal about your heart?

A Prayer
Father, I recognize that everything that I own is not my own, but yours. Help me to be a better manager of the resources you have entrusted to me, and show me how to order my finances in a way that honors and serves you. Help me to establish patterns in my life now that will serve my family and others well. Thank you, Lord, for trusting me with your resources. Amen.

Chapter 16

Develop a Sound Body

As you consider the resources and assets that the Lord has given you, one of the greatest gifts you have is your own physical body. Your body is one of the only things that you will get just one of in life. You only get one. Yet it is interesting to me to see how so many guys treat other assets they have in life better than their own bodies.

Your body needs your attention, and during this life on earth, you must learn to live peacefully in your body. After all, your very body is a temple of God. Your body is the very dwelling place where God has chosen to reside on earth. We cannot take this lightly, and we must learn what it means to honor and steward these temple tabernacles that each of us have been entrusted with, and your single years is a great time to create these habits.

To start, we should establish that God is more concerned about our hearts than he is about our physical bodies. First Samuel 16:7 tells us, "The Lord does not look at the things people look at. People look at the outward appearance, but the Lord looks at the heart" (NIV). At the same time, God has given you your body to live in during this short life on earth, and indeed, you cannot separate your spiritual, emotional, or relational life from your physical body. You should seek to be more concerned about your heart than your body, but you must take care of your body too.

For a lot of guys, I know there can be deep desires within you to achieve a certain type of body. It is good that you recognize that you have been given something and that you want to care for it, but I want to challenge you to be sure to check your motivation and reasoning for *why* you want a certain type of body.

For years, I worked hard to get six-pack abs. In a season where God was checking my motives for everything, I read Proverbs 16:2 which says, "All a person's ways seem pure to them, but motives are weighed by the Lord" (NIV). Many times, when I strive to improve my own physical fitness, my motive is in the wrong place. This can look like working out like crazy to achieve a body of my dreams just so that others will like me more. If you have lived for years seeking to desire a certain physical appearance, ask yourself, why do I want to look this certain way?

Christians must learn to have the right mindset toward our bodies, and at the same time we must weigh and evaluate our motives for how we desire to look. It's easy to hear the call to take care of your body and immediately think you need to have massive muscles to be living out this biblical command. But in reality, you just need a body that is able to do the work of the Lord and that will sustain and foster your spiritual, emotional, and relational life.

Paul tells us to "offer your bodies as a living sacrifice . . . to God" (Rom. 12:1 NIV). In the Old Testament, animals used for sacrifice were the best of the flock given to the Lord. We, too, should seek to order our bodies as healthy, ready, and nourished sacrifices unto the Lord.

What is your perspective on your body? Do you see your body as a tool for worship and a living sacrifice for God? Or do you instead see your body as a something irrelevant to your faith that you, not the Lord, have full autonomy over? We indeed are not our own, we were bought with a price, and we must honor God with our bodies (1 Cor. 6:19-20).

Your goal in your single season (or any other season of life) should be to best honor God with the resources he has currently entrusted you with. You must be careful to not sin in the name of honoring God and should ask for the guidance of the Holy Spirit to convict you and teach you how to best honor the body he has given you.

For some, that might look like auditing the foods that are going into your mouth and seeking to make some adjustments. For others, that might look like eliminating one session in the gym next week and choosing to serve and minister to others instead.

No matter where you are, it's always wise to seek to live a physically healthy lifestyle. Though you should ask the Lord to check your heart and motive behind this, your body is filled with potential to be a grand worshipping agent if you take care of it. Like most things in life, few things only effect only you. Your health affects the body of Christ. If you're healthy, you're able to offer your body to the service needs of others in your community. Similarly, if you're deeply overweight or have low energy because of your poor food choices, you rob others of being blessed by your service.

Your physical health also has the potential to affect your family. Many single guys will be a father one day, and for me, I would rather be in the ball game with my children than on the sidelines watching. What you do right now with your physical body will have an impact on your physical capabilities later in life.

Physical health effects other areas of our lives too. Research suggests exercise is known to boost your mood, combat disease and health conditions, promote better sleep, build discipline, and improve your [future] sex life.[22] Achieving a sound body is more than just mere appearance; it affects all areas of your life and will elevate your potential more than you think.

As you aim to become healthier physically, here are a couple of things for you to consider:

Have a Plan

Theologian Donald Whitney says, "Discipline without direction is drudgery."[23] How many times have you tried to discipline yourself to reach a goal or achieve success, yet failed at it? Was it because you didn't have a crystal-clear plan you could follow? Create a large, clear physical goal for yourself, write it down, and remind yourself of it often.

Start Small

A big mistake people make when they journey is that they set unrealistic expectations too soon, then when those expectations are unmet, they become discouraged and stop working toward a healthier version of themselves. Whether you are wanting to lose weight or just put on some more muscle, it's imperative to set small goals for yourself that can be met quickly. When you celebrate these small wins and successes in hitting your goal, you are more likely to set another goal and continue to push yourself further. Remember, big successes are often a combination of small wins.

Include Others

Goals are more likely to be met when you tell someone else what your goal is. Ask friends around you to consistently check in with you about your progress. Knowing that you will have friends ask you about your progress will keep you focused and help you avoid compromising or giving up. Telling others about your goal will also help you to regularly check your motives for striving to reach your goal.

If you want to be entrusted with big things in your life, you must be a good manager of the small things you have in front of you. Your physical body is one of life's greatest tests to see if you are willing to and prepared to take good care of what you already have.

Just as it can be tempting to allow small sins into our lives, it can also be tempting to allow small compromises in our physical health as well. It can be easy to justify fast food or dessert. While there's nothing wrong with occasional dessert and enjoying yourself, too many compromises can lead you miles away from your long-term goal.

One of the most encouraging principles I heard when I began an exercise program last year was, "Successful people do consistently what unsuccessful do occasionally."[24] Consistent compromises will lead to results you don't want. Give yourself grace and don't become legalistic, but seek to be disciplined in this area of your life. There will be days you don't feel like working out or days you want to drink that chocolate milkshake, but those small compromises will derail you from your bigger picture goals.[25] The success you have in achieving your physical goals will come from the many small honorable decisions that you make.

When Paul is writing to Timothy, he instructs Timothy to discipline himself for the purpose of godliness (1 Tim. 4:7–8). When you unpack the original text and examine the word *discipline* in the Greek language, you'll find he used the word *gymnasia*. Looking at this word, you can quickly notice that this is the root for our English word *gymnasium*. It is interesting to me that *discipline* and *gymnasium* are synonyms here. The discipline you are doing in your physical life in a gym can be reflected and mirrored into the spiritual disciplines you should practice too.

There is an inherent link between what you do to exercise and train yourself for a better physical body and what you do to become more godly and holy in your spiritual life. Think about it…if you follow Christ and truly believe that you are a temple of the Holy Spirit, shouldn't that lead you to treating and caring for your body differently?

If you lack discipline in your physical life, it is likely you lack discipline in your spiritual life too. If all you eat is junk food, then you might malnourish your spiritual life too. Creating the disciplines around your physical health and nutrition can propel you to be healthy with your spiritual life too. If you allow it, the degree of intentionality you implement in your fitness can be the same level of intentionality you demonstrate in your walk with the Lord as you grow deeper and closer to him.

Your body is not just a body. It is a hand-made gift given to you by the Creator of all things. It was made by the Creator for the glory of the Creator; our bodies are agents of worship to God. How we decide to conduct and manage our bodies reflects our appreciation (or lack of) of this gift from our Father.

As a single man, take the opportunity to wrestle with what it looks like for you to best honor God with the body that you have right now.

A Question
Do the activities that you do with your body more often serve you or others?

A Prayer
Lord, thank you for creating my body the way that you have and for entrusting me with it as a place where you dwell. Teach me to offer my body as a living sacrifice to you each day and convict me of the sinful

motives in my heart that seek to build my own image and kingdom rather than yours. Help me to include others as I work toward honoring you with everything.

Chapter 17

Labor Unconventionally

I was two months into my new corporate-America job when I began experiencing the desire to do something else. The job I had was doable, but I noticed early on that the work I was doing wasn't lining up with my passions, talents, or long-term goals nor with the dreams I had in mind. The work I was doing was by no means my dream job, and as I began to earn my paycheck, I wondered if it would be possible to make additional money in new ways.

One night I was eating dinner with my parents, and I informed them that I was considering applying to a part-time position at a grocery store just to make some extra cash. I tossed around the idea of delivering food, working as a barista, or even doing some odd jobs for my neighbors in town. Though my parents weren't opposed to me making some extra cash, they challenged me to use my natural talents in a different way and encouraged me to build a side-hustle.

As I remained in my full-time job, I began to ask the Lord for new possibilities. As I actively prayed, God began to pursue me with an idea. In May 2020 God gave me the idea and opportunity to use my experience in singleness as a platform to encourage and develop other single men. As I began to think about what this would look like, I realized I could spend my time on some of most favorite disciplines, such as writing content, teaching others, marketing and building a brand, and networking with others. So, I decided to give it a shot.

Slowly, I began to use the few minutes I had between meetings at my day job to develop a brand and platform circling around this new idea. Many people who opt into getting a full-time job right out of college wind up far from enjoying their role. Some people graduate from undergrad then pursue a master's degree and sit around wishing they could dive into work they actually love. So many of us hear the lie that we won't find work we love until our forties or fifties and that our younger years need to be spent enjoying life and doing fun things.

The reality is you are in a unique place in your life right now to pursue work that really matters to you. You don't need to wait until you quit your corporate job or until you reach age forty-five; you can pursue work you love right now, today. As a guy who is single, you are not burdened with providing for a family or many other obligations that might come later in life. With minimal responsibilities and requirements right now, what would it look like for you to start living out your purpose and operating within the strengths, talents, and passions God has given you?

I want to challenge you to take some risks and step out into a side-hustle, job, or hobby that you love. I'm not saying that you need to quit your day job, but don't wait three decades to step into work that really matters to you! Start right now while you are single and reap the lessons that will come with pursuing work that you love.

Here are a couple things I have learned from others as I've labored unconventionally.

Know Yourself

Just like you can't book plane tickets for vacation until you know whether you want to explore the mountains or the beach, you can't pursue a more meaningful or creative work until you know who you are and what you want. And more specifically, you need to know who you are and what your talents, skills, and passions are. God has given you a unique set of desires that no one else has, and you should use these as a guide for the work you pursue.

Take time to ask people you are close with what they think your talents and skills are. Take personality assessments or get coaching from a mentor to work on defining the person who you are.

As you gain clarity in how you are designed and where you function the greatest, you'll be able to be more selective and discerning in your pursuit for work that matters to you. Be sure that you don't just settle for any new side-hustle or part-time gig. I'm glad my parents talked me out of working at a grocery store! You might find yourself saying no a lot before you find yourself saying yes to a new opportunity. Try a vocation that actually means something to you and incorporates the unique characteristics God has designed in you.

Expand Your Network

Do you know anyone who is doing what you hope to do one day? Is there someone in your neighborhood who has your dream job, or is there someone on the other side of the country who is well known and a professional at what you want to do one day? You increase your likelihood of stepping into a dream position or starting a side hustle you're passionate about when you surround yourself with people who are already doing it.

As I began working on my own side-hustle, I connected with dozens of men and women who were doing similar work. I emailed people, met some people for lunch, spent time on video calls, and did anything I could just to spend a few minutes picking someone else's brain. Not only were these men and women extremely encouraging to me, they gave me advice, showed me what I was doing wrong and even connected me with others in the industry.

With technology, we have the ability to notice and get connected to the people who are already doing what we love to do. Step outside your comfort zone and ask someone to coffee, lunch, or to connect for a few minutes online. I like to pull the "Hey, I'm a young guy who is starting off in his career" card when I email someone asking for advice. Even with qualifications, experience, knowledge, and passion, there is no substitute for relationships. Make it a priority even if you aren't looking to pivot in your career or begin a side hustle. Get connected to other men and women who are doing similar work as you. It's way easier than you think, and you never know what you'll gain from these conversations.

Start Small

Truett Cathy, founder of Chick-fil-A, often said "You can't succeed if you don't start."[26] Many people want the fruits of the labor without doing any of the labor.

It is not so much that people are scared of doing the labor, but instead that they are not really sure where to begin. When starting a side hustle, there is often a big dream or goal in mind, and as it seems almost impossible to reach, people just opt not to begin.

As you consider your own side-hustle, simply getting started is the best way to begin. When I created this ministry, I had no idea what I was doing, but I kept telling myself I am going to do it anyways. Taking the first step is challenging because it involves breaking fear, taking risks, and using some of your own resources.

And the truth is, the first thing you create most likely won't be something you're proud of. My entrepreneurship professor Jim Corman in college used to tell us, "Your first prototype should be your ugly duckling; you won't be proud of it." When I first started creating content, I wasn't proud of how great my works were, but instead I was proud that I had decided to start. No one is ever good at anything the first time around, so it's key that you start now. When you release the first version of your product or service, it should be the bare minimum. It won't have all the bells and whistles you want it to have one day. If you're embarrassed by the first drafts of your service or product you are putting into the market, you know you are heading in the right direction.

The truth is you are in a unique time in your life right now to pursue work that really matters. As you begin to understand yourself, expand your network, and start small, new opportunities will arise for you, and you will gain insight and clarity in how to best approach your future.

You might also realize that as you start something new you might need to become more qualified in that trade. When I began writing new content frequently and speaking into biblical manhood and discipleship, I decided I needed more training under my belt, so I enrolled in seminary classes to help me build my knowledge and gain more tools to be more faithful within the work that I love to do. You might need to take some night classes, find someone to teach you a skill, or watch content online.

Many men remain in jobs they hate just so that they can provide for their children and family, but as a single man right now, you don't have this burden! You have freedom right now, and you have the chance to work unconventionally unlike any other season of your life.

What's that dream job you have always wanted to pursue? What is that side hustle you've considered starting sometime? Get started today and reframe your single years as a new kind of pursuit.

There are many men who have used their season of singleness to start something unique and purposeful. My friend Ben used his extra time in his mid-twenties to start a new church in the Atlanta area where he is now the lead pastor and inspires his church to serve the city. My friend Taylor in his early thirties used the extra time he had apart from his day job to write a book, which has since evolved into several series. My friend David noticed a passion he had for coffee and for helping others, so at age twenty-four he opened up a coffeeshop in the downtown area of his hometown where customers can determine the dollar amount they pay for their drinks.

Don't get caught in the trap of working a job you hate for your entire adult life in which you're counting down the minutes until you can retire. Your specific situation right now in your life might be the very best situation in which to grow your own new adventure. As risky as trying and starting something new may sound, you are in the best place in your life right now as a single man to take the risk. Pursue work that really matters to you. Go "all-in" and learn, develop, and grow more in a profession that matters to you. You never know how the small things you do in this season could having lasting ROI for you in the future.

A Question

As you try to figure out your talents and skills, ask yourself, "During and after what activity am I most alive and energized?" or "What do other people say that I am good at?"

A Prayer

Lord, thank you for the opportunity I have to live on this earth during such a time as this. I pray that you would allow me to use my single season wisely and empower me to begin to pursue work that aligns with the skills, talents, and passions that you have given me. Amen.

Chapter 18

Initiate Community

In the age of increasing technology and the ability to do most things from our smart devices, the need to talk face-to-face throughout the day has declined.

When I was living in the downtown area of a large city, I quickly became immersed in the convenience technology provided. I worked an eight-hour day on my laptop at home. I ordered my groceries from my phone. I could workout in my bedroom from a video I found online. I truly had everything I needed in my own 900-square-foot high rise apartment.

Everything except people.

It didn't take long for me to notice the side effects of a life lived like this. I experienced increased anxiety, poor social skills, and a lack of motivation for work as I enjoyed all the convenient options I had at my fingertips. I found myself not enjoying life like I once had and even giving back into sins that I thought I had overcome.

People in the United States have, for decades, prided themselves on personal independence and self-sufficiency and on being able to get things done without the need for others in their life, but an increase in efficiency and accomplishments does not warrant a fulfilling life. In fact, people who isolate themselves just to achieve the next success are destined to yield a life of discontentment, unsatisfaction, and frustration.

Now, I don't know about you, but I like to get stuff done. I love a good checklist, and fewer things bring me greater joy than checking things off the list. But one of my biggest struggles in life to this day is my inclination to eliminate conversations in order to get things done faster. Doing this has led me to learn the hard way that not investing in others and not allowing them to invest in me is the shortest path to burnout. I have to tell myself that instead of becoming frustrated with interruptions, I need to remember that the work I do and the ministry I partake in is always more fruitful when I am rooted in community.

Humans are designed to be social creatures; we know this because we know our Creator. God himself is a community; he is made up of three persons: the Father, the Son, and the Holy Spirit. God is highly relational, and as he created humans in his own image, he imprinted the requirement for relationships on everyone's life. Avoiding people and removing yourself from community is running contrary to the way in which you were created to function.

So many single guys today are outrageously lonely. What bothers me is that most of these guys like to blame someone else for their loneliness. You hear things like, "The church never has events for guys my age," or "All my friends are always too busy." Today many men are lonely but want someone else to fix their problem.

In your single years, you have an incredible opportunity to initiate community. In fact, you will have the need for wholesome community until you leave this earth, so your single season gives you an impressive chance to intentionally develop solid relationships that will last a lifetime.

My college pastor Miles Fidell says, "God has rigged Christianity to be relational."[27] There is no way around community in your life. The greatest opportunities, victories, lessons, and adventures in your life will begin with the people you have around you.

Every human being needs to belong, and you need to belong too. You need guys in your life who know you, know your story, know your past, know your future goals, know your sin struggles, and know your likes and your dislikes. Having men in your life who deeply care about you and for you is critical in your life as a single guy.

You need men in your life who will challenge you. In a recent small group that I was a part of, I became convicted that I was not stewarding the God-given talents I had well because I was fearful of what others thought of me. I noticed that I was selfishly keeping my giftings to myself instead of growing Christ's kingdom. I would have never realized this if it weren't for a group of people calling me out on this. You need people who will challenge you to be the best version of yourself you can possibly be.

As you stand at the intersection of many decisions you have in life, God is likely to use the people around you to communicate his will to you. God has always been in the business of using others to communicate on his behalf, and I've seen him continue to do the same in the midst of some of my biggest decisions I have made in my life.

You need men in your life who will fight with you. Every single one of us is going through something right now. A sin. A breakup. Uncertainty about the future. There is never a time in your life or in the lives of the people around you where we are not navigating uncertain waters. The people around you will give you new perspectives, offer encouragement, speak wisdom, and provide comfort for whatever season of life you are in right now.

When I launched my first book, I had no idea that I had a faithful friend praying for me quietly in the background. I remember when my book launched how tempted I was to have great pride and arrogance, yet somehow, I felt a humble spirit over me that was anchored in gratitude to the Lord. Later I found out that this was the prayer of my friend in the background. I credit some of my greatest victories in life to some of the strongest prayers that others have prayed over me.

Whether you need to rethink the people you are surrounding yourself with right now or you're noticing you are lacking fruitful community in your life, there are three things you can begin doing in your life now to begin to initiate community:

Go Deep, Not Wide

There is wisdom in going deep with few people rather than wide with many people. I made this mistake in college when I knew hundreds of people, yet none of them really knew me. Though knowing many people is valuable and has its place, the reality is, you can't be close to everyone.

Out of the twelve disciples Jesus had, he was closest to three of them—

Peter, James, and John. It is wise to have a core group of people that know you intimately. Have your community of a few guys and be content. There will be many people in your life whom you won't have the capacity to develop deep relationships with, so be content with the intentionality you share between a small group of brothers. It is through these few deep relationships that you experience the great fruits of friendship.

Start with a few guys from your church, a singles ministry in your area, your gym, or your workplace, and begin to be intentional about growing a relationship with them. If you have a large circle of friends already, find the friends who you can go deep with and be intentional to grow and develop these relationships.

Be Persistent

Community will not happen overnight. Miles Fidell says that "the price of community is the sacrifice of commitment,"[28] so as you seek to establish authentic and meaningful relationships in your life, be sure to give yourself grace when you aren't seeing the type of community you hope for right away.

So many guys are eager for community, yet very few have the courage to initiate it. Be bold and be the guy in your community to take the initiative to facilitate relationships.

Initiate community through small steps and be patient as a new friendship compounds into something greater down the road. Continuously try new things to cultivate community with others. As establishing community proves to be challenging at times, you'll be tempted to give up and do life on your own. Remind yourself of the value friends have on your life and how necessary community is for you.

Have Boundaries

Don't be afraid to say "no" to some friendships in your life. It might do some of us some good if we cut out a few of the friends who have a lot of influence in our life right now. You will become like those who you are around. If the people around you are putting negative thoughts, ideas, and words into your life, then you will quickly be negative too. If your friends are life-giving with words of encouragement, honesty, and hard work, then you'll likely do the same.

Remember that a friendship is a two-way street, meaning you need a friend who you can communicate with authentically and who you allow to do the same toward you. If you don't feel commitment from someone, it is okay to move on and find someone else you can go deeper with.

When I felt the Lord call me to start seminary a few years ago, I began to establish my community and network by connecting online with business and ministry leaders in the area. I would reach out to someone on social media and explain to them that I was a twenty-five-year-old about to move to their city, and I wanted to hear some advice and wisdom from them about what to get involved in this new town. Before I knew it, I was hopping on video calls from people all around the city. They each began to connect me other men and women in the area. Within a month of moving there, I had dozens of relationships with local adults I could go to for support, questions, and advice. Be creative in how you form new relationships and don't believe the lie that people don't want to connect to you.

Many people regret not having life-giving friendships in their lives, but I've never heard someone complain about having meaningful community. You are in charge of the community in your life. If you do become married one day, you will continue to have the responsibility to initiate community within your family and for your family, so it is best to begin growing in this skill now as a single guy.

A Question

Who has the loudest voice in your life? Are they pointing you toward holiness and becoming more like Christ? Do they know you, challenge you, and fight with you?

A Prayer

God, I understand that you have created me to need community. I recognize that I grow best in community and that through others, I may notice hear will and receive your guidance. Help me to be bold in initiating community during this season of my life and teach me to go deep with a small group of guys. Thank you for providing for me in this way. Amen.

Chapter 19

Develop Leadership

It's easy to read the word *leadership* and think it is irrelevant or unapplicable to our lives. Leadership is the CEO of the company or the pastor at church, right? But as my dad likes to say, "Everyone is always leading at least one person. Themselves!"

The truth is you are a leader. And every leader must grow in his character and in his competency throughout a lifetime. You see, no leader has it figured out, but many leaders have indeed spent intentional time and money on developing who they are as a leader.

Developing the leader within you is a very important task to do. In fact, I would argue that it is not a task that you can afford to neglect! Whether you are leading just yourself or multitudes of people, taking the time to develop yourself as a leader will benefit everyone.

Growing yourself as a leader is also important because if you are blessed with a wife one day, you will be given the opportunity to lead her. And if you have kids, you will be the person who leads your family. God specifically designed marriage to function with the male as the head and this is not a duty that can be taken lightly or passively.

It's interesting to see how powerful things are when they are done God's way. The power and influence a man has over his family is staggering. A survey found that if a child is the first person in a household to become a Christian, there is a 3.5 percent probability that everyone else in the household will follow. If the mother is the first to become a Christian, there is a 17 percent probability that everyone else in the household will follow. However, when the father is first, there is a 93 percent probability everyone else in the household will follow.[29] The role of a father in a family is critical, and leading your family well is important.

Starting to develop your leadership now while you are single will help you to be more prepared and equipped for the more challenging levels of leadership down the road.

It's always funny to me how I think I am the best person to lead myself. Here I am trying to lead the most difficult and stubborn person in my life, but I do it alone. Trying to lead myself is like trying to drive from one end of the country to the other, yet I don't bother using GPS and instead rely on my own knowledge.

John Maxwell says, "It's hard to improve when you have no one but yourself to follow."[30] When we rely only on ourselves, we limit the potential that we have. When we use only ourselves for the input we receive, the only output we reap is what we know.

You've heard the saying before that more is caught rather than taught, which means that people tend to learn more through observation of others rather than knowledge taught pedantically to them. I have found this to be profoundly true in my life. One of the best ways to grow in your leadership is to establish models who can guide and counsel you. The truth is, no matter where you are seeking to grow, you need people to follow. Models are the people who will inspire, guide, and correct your path as you begin to navigate into the future seasons of your life.

When I realized that all the knowledge I had from college would only get me so far in life, I decided I needed to start to observe some men who were doing what I wanted to do one day. In 2020, I became an expert at following some of the greatest leaders across different industries. I caught lessons from these guys and observed everything there was to observe from each of them. When I started to follow high caliber people, learn the lessons they were teaching, and implement the habits they preached, I started to see my life take off.

Every man needs both masters and mentors in his life to help his leadership grow.

Masters

Finding masters in your life means putting yourself around the people who are living in your dream job. Sometimes these people might be well known in culture, but many times they are not. These are the men who are doing what you want to do one day. These guys are in your dream job, dream company, dream career, and are deeply passionate and focused on what they are doing.

You don't even have to personally know the master in order to learn from them. Many times, there are resources from these types of people, such as books, online courses, podcasts, articles, and interviews for you to take advantage of today.

Consuming content and spending time with masters has led to me some of my greatest successes in my life so far. As a young man, it is easy to get discouraged when others my age are not doing what I am doing and are pursuing the wrong things during their single years, but staying plugged into the mission and goals for my life through the inspiration from effective leaders is a key ingredient for me in staying set on the course.

Mentors

Mentors are the men in your life who can intentionally and diligently pour into you on a regular basis. These men might not be in your dream job or your own preferred industry, but it certainly does help if they are. These are the men in your local communities who are faithful in their walk with the Lord, diligent in leading their own families, and are demonstrating effectiveness and satisfaction in the workplace.

These men are the ones who will sit down with you multiple times a year to provide spiritual, professional, and relational advice. They will help you set goals, push you to step outside of your comfort zone, and help to reveal any blind spots you might have. No man is immune to the need of someone like this in his life.

In my experience, the best way to find these guys are at your local church. Reach out to the staff at your church and ask them if they are aware of any solid older men who might be willing to disciple and lead another young man.

There is an illusion in our culture and the church that there is not anyone available to mentor individuals because everyone is too busy. The truth is, there are a lot of older men out there who are seeking to pour into someone younger than them, they just don't know who to pour into!

The next step to finding this person in your life is you taking the first step. Many people wait for a mentor to ask if they would like to be discipled, but you need to take the first step and ask someone to mentor you.

As the man in the driver seat of your life, it's your responsibility to steer yourself toward people who can help your leadership grow. There are many people who allow life to happen to them, and then there are the successful people who "happen to life" by controlling the inputs that feed their minds. You have a choice on the voices that speak into you, and it's my challenge to you to actively and diligently pursue these voices that can help you live and lead a more meaningful and significant life.

In the single season you are in right now, you must develop your leadership. You have an incredible opportunity to establish healthy and purposeful relationships with godly men. Putting these relationships into place today in your life will help you to continue this vital habit throughout the rest of your life. You will always need the masters and mentors in your life, no matter when or if you get married, how successful you become, or how much money you have.

As you initiate and approach these relationships in your life, keep in mind that the people who are pouring into you are humans too, and they will make mistakes. Perfection is not found in any human, and demanding that the people in your life not be subject to mistakes is setting yourself up for disappointment. Have grace with others, even those you respect the most.

As I have tried to grow myself as a leader, I have found that the best model is the man Jesus, who spent thirty years on planet earth almost two thousand years ago. With the abundance of records we have from his life, there are countless lessons to be observed from his actions, words, and relationships with others. Though Jesus is no longer on earth physically, we have access to him through prayer and by reading the accounts documented in Scripture about his life.

What is great about setting Jesus as your number one model is that he is the best mentor because he created you and he knows the plans he has for each day of your future. He has given you the best advice throughout the entire book of the Bible, and he loves you deeply more than any other human being could.

As your relationship with Jesus becomes more established and grows, your relationships with other godly men will become more meaningful and purpose filled. The best way to have a successful mentorship with men is to allow yourself to be mentored by the one and only Jesus Christ and to allow him to teach you the best leadership lessons, reveal your purpose for your life to you, and show his love toward you to encourage you as press on to pursuing what matters most.

A Question

What are your desires and aspirations for a career one day? Who can you read about, listen to, or interview who has lived out your dream job or is currently doing so?

A Prayer

Lord, thank you for the ability I have to grow and change. Please help me connect to the right men who will be able to lead, shepherd, and guide me in my current season. Help me to receive truth from these men and steward their council well. Amen.

Chapter 20

Export the Gospel

I am grateful to have been a Christian for more than ten years of my life. When I reflect on what having a personal relationship with Jesus has done for me, I am quickly overcome with gratitude and joy for all the comfort, security, and peace that Christ brings me.

When we look out into the world, most people globally do not have this same hope. It wasn't until the last two years that God began to work in my heart to cultivate a heart of compassion for the people in our world who do not believe in Jesus Christ as king.

It's easy to think that it is the work of a missionary to share the gospel. In one sense, that's true, but it's not just the missionary who is given this charge. All people who believe in Jesus Christ as their Lord and Savior are given the task to share the hope they possess with others.

John Piper says it this way, "Missions exist because worship does not."[31] Christians should be so filled with awe of God that they naturally share the gospel with those around them from the wonder and love inside of them. In fact, a sign that you are growing in your closeness and intimacy with the Lord and in your love for him can be reflected in the way you share the gospel with others.

I've lived most of my Christian life scared to share the good news with anyone. I was hiking with a buddy one day when he deeply convicted me that me not sharing the gospel either meant I really didn't believe the gospel was true or that I really didn't love my neighbors enough to share the gospel with them. Ouch! He was right. As I have spent hours and hours building and growing my relationship with God over the last several years, it has been amazing to watch how naturally sharing the gospel can become.

Sharing the gospel is an act of obedience for a Christian, but this act serves far greater than just a mere act of obligation. Sharing the gospel challenges us in a way that makes us truly dependent on God. Sometimes when I share the gospel with others, I don't know what to say, and in desperation I rely on the Holy Spirit to give me the best words to say (see Luke 12:11-12). Sharing this hope with others also helps to reaffirm our beliefs and challenges us to understand God and his Word more fully.

Being single gives you an incredible opportunity to share what you believe with others. God has used single men and women for centuries to advance his kingdom in mighty ways. Sharing the gospel takes time and availability, which you likely have as a single guy.

I want to challenge you to leverage your single years as a platform for sharing the gospel with others. Begin by building relationships with non-believers and leverage the trust and relational equity you build as a platform to share about Jesus.

As you set out to do this, I think you might find that with a little creativity, you can create some serious momentum for sharing the hope that you possess. Here are three things you can do this week:

Open up Your Home

Whether you live in a dorm, apartment, or a house, God has given you a place where you can facilitate gatherings. You don't need a big place, just a room with some chairs and a table will work. Sharing the gospel is about creating spaces where gospel-centered conversations can take place. When you invite non-believers to your home, you create an opportunity to share the gospel. Even bringing people to your house to build a relationship with them is a win.

Try to create a rhythm of opening your home consistently. Could you have people over for a game night every Monday? Or what about a Waffle Night on the first Wednesday of every month? You could open your home up to watch football games on Saturday or Sundays. The idea is to find a way to create a predictable pattern for the nonbeliever of when he can come over to your home.

Re-order Your Routine

In our world today, it is so easy to go throughout our day with minimal human contact. This has its conveniences, but unfortunately, these conveniences eliminate our opportunity to engage with a lost world. Can you try to find ways in your day-to-day errands to start conversation with people?

For me, this has looked like using the regular check-out lines at the grocery store rather than using self-checkout so that I can talk to the clerk behind the counter. Maybe it looks like paying for your gas inside the gas station instead of at the pump or hand delivering one of your utility bills. Finding ways to come in contact with people with the hopes of building a relationship and sharing the gospel will take intentionality in your life. Are you up for the challenge?

Caring for Nonbelievers

As you think about building new relationships with nonbelievers throughout your local area, you want to take your relationships deeper with these people by extending care. One way you can show love toward lost friends is by praying for them often. Pray for their salvation and for their heart to be desperate for a Savior and for them to die to their own pride one day and submit to Christ. In addition to prayer, you can also serve the nonbelievers in your life too. Could you bring a meal over to your friend's house? What about sending them some money on Venmo for a coffee? Or offering to do some sort of house- or yardwork for them. The hope is that your unbelieving friends will notice the love of Christ shining through you and eventually ask you about the hope that you have.

Discipling others takes intentionality. It does not happen by itself, and it will not just naturally happen later in your life. Sharing the gospel with others and making disciples of Christ starts with you being faithful with the small resources that God has given you and leveraging these for gospel conversations. If you want your faith to grow, challenge yourself to have spiritual conversations with people.

I've been inspired by how some of my friends try to live missionally and share the gospel as they go. My friend Eli has used his single years to take two days a month to walk around his college campus and strike up spiritual conversations with others. My friend Syler has started taco nights at his (small) college apartment to get to know his neighbors more. My friend Jonathan makes it a point to start conversations in the sauna at his gym since the guys in there are usually willing to sit and talk. And my friend Christian has no shame in walking up to people on the streets on Sunday morning inviting them to his church down the road.

I used to be so intimidated by what others would think of me if I began to talk about spirituality with someone. I have realized that people are not as hostile toward the gospel as I had often assumed they would be. I realized that people are in desperate need of direction, wisdom, and hope in their lives, and they have likely already learned that the things of the world cannot provide them the hope that they do deeply long for. Having these conversations reinforced my faith and gave me energy and passion for Jesus Christ I had never seen before.

Be bold and make it a point in your single years to intentionally create spaces to share the gospel with others!

A Question

What are some ways you can sacrifice convenience so that you can strike up a conversation with someone?

A Prayer

Lord, thank you that you have entrusted me with your good news. I realize that I have missed opportunities to share the gospel with others in the past, and I am asking you to give me a spirit of confidence and trust in you to engage with others. Help me to be bold about sharing the hope that I possess. Amen.

Chapter 21

Enjoy and Explore

I hope you are growing in your eagerness to take full ownership of your single season. Singleness can be fun and it can be such a platform for massive growth in your life too.

If you're like me or most men, you're ready to fix the problem. You're ready to tackle some of the problems that you see in your own life and begin taking charge of the season of life God has placed you in. This is a great thing!

Owning your single season takes intentionality and grit, but I don't want you to become so consumed with seeing results of satisfaction and life change that you forget to actually enjoy this season of life God has placed you in. My dad once told me, "Any season of life is fun if you make it fun." These simple words have stuck with me and have been motivation for me to take time to actually enjoy the seasons of life God has placed me in.

God has gifted humans with the ability to enjoy life. Even on a sinful and broken planet, God still desires for humans to find joy and pleasure and we should make it a point to enjoy this gift.

Singleness gives you the opportunity do things in life that other seasons do not allow. Nine years ago when I was crafting my personal mission statement, I made sure to include the word *explore* because I wanted to emphasize that my single years were going to be filled with exploring. Exploring is one of the great things that being single allows you to do.

As a single guy, I have taken two one-month long trips to Europe where I had the privilege of exploring over twenty countries. I have been to a dozen other countries around the world on mission trips, business trips, and vacations, making my number of countries visited thirty-five to date. I've had a blast taking long road trips around the US with friends and alone, and I have enjoyed some of the most incredible points of interest around the country.

As a single guy, you have the opportunity to start and try new hobbies in your life too. When I was twenty-six, I bought my first house and began to fix it up and do some improvements on it. It was challenging, but in doing so I learned so much about houses, tools, decorations, and which aisle PVC pipe is on at Home Depot. I've also taken up CrossFit and weightlifting, soap making, an online clothing brand, writing, and so much more as a single guy. Singleness gives us so many opportunities to do new things.

Now, I don't want you just doing a bunch of random activities just to merely do them. Instead, find something that you actually enjoy doing and stick with it! I can assure you that when I started making soap, I thought this was going to be the next big business idea, but I wasn't a huge fan of all the meticulous measuring and methods that were required in the soap making process. I encourage you try a lot of different things, but only stick with the hobbies you love.

Seek to find ways to intentionally enjoy your single life. Enjoying singleness helps you to be content with where you are in life, and it helps eliminate the temptation to compare your life with others'. Enjoying where you are right now also shows God that you are honoring the gifts he gave you and are willing to multiply what he has entrusted to you.

Take ownership of this time. Show God that you are grateful for where he has divinely placed you in life. Show God you are willing to step outside of your comfort zone and die to your own pride in an attempt to honor him with the things he has blessed you with. Get creative and explore and enjoy your single life!

A Question

What can you do to enjoy this season of life God has placed you in?

A Prayer

Lord, thank you for the gift of enjoyment. I pray that in this season you have placed me in right now that I would not have shame about enjoying it. Help me to balance disciplines and personal growth while also taking time to explore and enjoy my single years. Amen.

Chapter 22

Pursue in Prayer

It was not until the first month of the pandemic in the United States that I noticed the opportunity of pursuing my future through the means of prayer. I had grown up praying, but most of my prayers consisted of me asking God (or, telling him) to bless the chicken nuggets I was about to eat or to help me get an A on a test I was unprepared to take. Praying over my future diligently was foreign to me, but it is something that I have continued to do until today.

One of the personal values I try to live by each day is to be proactive rather than reactive. To be proactive is to be thinking, planning, and engaging in advance so that you might be prepared to the fullest extent before something takes place. On the other hand, being reactive involves solving problems, issues, and dilemmas after they occur; it is to react to whatever happens. As I try to be a good steward of the time, energy, and money God has given me, I have found it far more beneficial to be proactive.

In your single season, you have the unique opportunity to prepare for your future through the means of prayer. As you understand that you will not be in the season of life you are in right now forever, you can begin to prepare for your next season of life through the means of prayer. As you remain rooted where God has you right now and stay faithful to the lessons he is teaching you, peeking into your future through prayer is one of the best ways to approach your future.

In my book *The Prayerful Pursuit*, I write about the four reasons why you should consider integrating the habit of prayer in your daily life. Consider these as you seek to integrate this key ingredient in your life.

First you should pray because we are commanded to pray in Scripture. Second, prayer tests our faith in God and helps us trust God. Next, prayer, unlocks God's plan for your life as each day of your life has already been planned out by God; by praying you bring God's will into being. Finally, one should adopt prayer in his life because it anchors your relationship to God and reminds you how dependent on God and desperate for God you really are.

As you begin to understand the purpose of prayer, you will see the meaning of prayer unfold in your life too. For many of my single years, I did not see the value in praying until I began to understand the purposes behind prayer. As I started to see the purposes behind prayer, my prayers changed, and they pivoted greatly from my traditional, dry, routine prayers into new, creative, bold prayers over my life.

As a single man, you have an unbelievable opportunity to build the habit of prayer into your life and to see the fruits that yield from the different purposes of prayer. You have control over the hours in your day, so you are able to integrate meaningful conversations with the Lord that will deepen your relationship with him. Praying is essential no matter what season of life you find yourself in, but in your single years, you have more control of your time and the ability to prayer more often.

One of the best ways to pray is to pray through a specific passage in Scripture. God's words help you to organize your thoughts and add clarity to what you should be petitioning God for. Even though every Bible verse is not a promise to you specifically, like it may have been to whom it was written, Scripture is filled with reminders of what his children are able to ask for from the Good Father. As you spend your daily time alone with the Lord, find a verse in his Word that you can begin to pray over your life. If you aren't sure where to start, the book of Psalms offers a wide variety of praise, pleas, and prayers to God that you can begin to adopt and speak in your life.

When I began to discover the meaning that prayer had in my life, I prayed prayers I had never prayed before. I think God has allowed many single men to be single so that they may pursue what is good through the means of prayer. As you begin to reframe your single season as a time to pray unconventionally, you can think about these three different areas of your life to pray over.

Prayers for Yourself

Before you can lead others, you must be able to lead yourself. To help others find freedom in their own lives, you need to find freedom in yours. I have spent much of my single life asking God to search me, refine me, and stretch me so that I may grow to the greatest potential in my current season.

Some of the requests you might ask of God during this time are:
- To operate from your true identity found in Jesus (Rom. 8:15)
- For a community of brothers for accountability and to call out unholiness in your life (James 5:16)
- For wisdom as you face challenging decisions (Eph. 5:15-17)
- For the Holy Spirit to make known any offensive way within you (Psalm 139:23)
- To cultivate a continual spirit of gratitude (Psalm 7:17)
- To discover and faithfully use your spiritual gifts (Romans 12:4-6)

Prayers for Others

Someone once told me the kindest thing you can do for somebody is to pray for them. In your life right now, you have space to lift others up to the Lord and to intercede on their behalf. Do you have friends who are in need right now? Do you know someone who is going through a stressful time or someone who has not been pursuing the Lord as much as you had hoped? When it seems like you don't have the right words to offer somebody in challenging times or when it seems like someone won't listen to a thing you say, the best thing you can do is to pray for that person.

In the Christian world, it is very easy to say "I'll be praying for you" to someone whom we know needs it, but with prayer, it isn't the thought that counts. Your friends and family need you to be fighting on your knees in prayer for them. Even if you know they aren't praying for you, making requests to the Lord on their behalf is one of the most self-sacrificing ways to give and to serve someone else. Your friends need your prayers, and you need your friends' prayers, and there is simply no substitute for it. Maybe God has planned that your friend's breakthrough is on the other side of your diligent prayers.

Prayers for "Her" and Marriage

Though there will be men who remain single for the duration of their lives, many men will end up marrying one day. In preparation for this season that many of us know is ahead, you should begin to pray for your future wife and for your marriage together.

If it is God's will for you is to get married, your wife is likely out there walking around in the world somewhere. That's a wild thought! Why not start praying for her life today? You don't have to wait until you're married or until you meet her to start praying for her. Surely, she is facing some of the same challenges you are facing today, and she could use prayers from her future husband.

Seasons of life will come where you begin to date and wonder what the timeline of this relationship should be and when you should move toward marriage. Surely the season is coming when you do become married, and you will face challenges in your life you have never faced before. Having children, purchasing a home, and growing in your career are all great possibilities on the horizon of your life, and in my opinion the best time to pray for these events is right now, before they happen. Spend some time thinking about the future seasons that are possible in life and ask the Lord to bless the time that is to come.

When I wrote *The Prayerful Pursuit*, each of the seventy-five different prayers stemmed from the very prayers I was praying over my own life. For several months, God was showing me different verses to pray over my own life, my future wife's life, and the future seasons of life I may have. I would highly encourage you to create a journal specifically for your prayers and begin to write down some of the requests you make to God. It's stunning to look back on my prayer journal from just a few years ago and already see the fruits that have come from those prayers. As you trace the blessings you experience in your life back to the prayers you offered to God, you will not only strengthen your own faith, but you will bring God the most glory that he deserves through praise and thanksgiving.

As you remain rooted and fully present in the season of life God has you in right now, you still know that your future is coming as each day moves on. Pursuing your future in prayer is one of the greatest opportunities God allows for during this single season. Though we are never guaranteed our future, we steward the time God has given us and may give us through the means of prayer.

A Question
Which friends or family members can you dedicate yourself to praying for?

A Prayer
Lord, thank you for the opportunity to come before you and petition things to you. God, I ask that you help me to cultivate a life that is marked by prayer. Would I be the man who prays first, before all things, and would you inspire me to pray bold, creative, and righteous prayers? Amen.

PART FOUR
Pursue Wisely

Chapter 23

What Is this Whole Pursuing Thing?

Your entire life is one giant pursuit.

For the Christian man, our lives are orchestrated around cultivating and pursuing a life of holiness and intimacy with our Lord. That is our pursuit. This can look different for every single person. Since every man is created differently and has his own unique sins and struggles, pursuing God in the context of a man's brokenness will look slightly different for everyone. But ultimately, the life of a Christian is beautifully centered around pursuing Jesus in our mundane, everyday life and seeking to align our will with God's.

When it comes to having a relationship with a woman, a Christian man must make it a point to continue to pursue God with his full heart before and during a relationship. This is why the pursuit of God during our single years is so important. If you do not know how to pursue God now as a single guy, then you will struggle to include God in your marriage. Our single years should be characterized by a life committed unto the Lord. This time should be full-on pursuit of Him.

As many guys are, indeed, not called to a life of singleness and desire to be in a relationship with a woman one day, there are many genuine questions that guys have as they consider starting a relationship:

- Am I called to marriage?
- Am I ready for a relationship?
- Is God's will for me to marry a woman?
- Is God's will for me to marry *that* woman?

- What if God's will is for me to marry that other woman?

Here's the thing: no matter how daunting and consequential these questions may be, the answer will come as you live a life of going all-in where God has you as a single guy. If you have done most of what this book has suggested, finding the answers to some of these questions should come quickly, naturally, and confidently.

The best thing you can do to pursue a woman is to pursue the Lord. Full-on. Nonstop.

If you take the time to uncover your identity and discover what is true about you according to God's Word, you will likely be more confident and secure as you pursue a woman. If you take the time to find freedom from some of your past struggles and sins, you will be a healthier person who is able to think, reason, and pursue a woman more confidently. Noticing opportunities that singleness allows shows God that you are taking ownership of this season of life and helps you to be content with where God has placed you.

Our lives are not about us. Indeed, God does not need us to sustain himself. Thus, our lives must be bent around the charge to submit to God's own will and desires in order that we may bring him the glory that he deserves. Submitting yourself to the desires of God within singleness is one of the best ways to indicate to God that you desire his will above your own.

In Matthew 25, Jesus told the story of a man who gave gold to three of his servants. To one servant he gave five bags worth, to another two, and to another one. The man left for a long time, then when he returned he asked his servants what they had each done with the gold that he had entrusted to them. The servant who was given five bags said he had deposited the gold and earned interest on the deposit, doubling the gold. The servant with the two bags of gold did the same thing and ended up with four bags because of the interest he had accrued on his investment. However, the servant with one bag said that he had buried the one bag of gold in the ground to protect it and keep it safe. Jesus tells us that the man was well pleased with the servants who had doubled their treasures. He said to them, "Well done, good and faithful servant! You have been faithful with a few things; I will put you in charge of many things. Come and share your master's happiness!" But to the one who had buried his treasure, the man was very disappointed in him and demanded that his one bag of gold be given to the man with ten bags.

We are called to invest the treasures God has given us into opportunities that bring God more glory. He has given you a few bags of gold in this season of singleness, and you have the opportunity to multiply these treasures. Having a wife is a gift, and God will entrust us with a marriage as we prove to be faithful with the small things he has given us. Your pursuit of a woman starts with your pursuit of God.

A Question
What was my motive in reading this book? Was it to submit to God's will for my life or to assert my own agenda and plan? Am I at a place where I ultimately want God's will to be done in my life?

A Single Shift
Ask a friend if they think you are ready to date someone. Communicate to your friend your motivations and desires for wanting to date.

A Prayer
Lord, as I consider pursuing a woman, help me to continue maximizing the treasures that you have given me. Convict me if I put another person before you and teach me to prioritize pursuing you continuously within the context of a relationship. Amen.

Chapter 24

Pursuing Like Christ

You've heard it said before: Men are the ones who are supposed to pursue in a relationship. But why do men pursue? Quite simply, it boils down to following Jesus's lead. As men of God, what better person to learn from than our Lord and Savior Jesus Christ?

Jesus had a bride. This bride was not a woman, but instead the Bible tells us that Jesus's bride was the church. Men should learn how to pursue their brides as Christ pursued the church.

When Jesus pursued his bride, he did so as an act of love. Jesus loved his bride so deeply that he gave his life up for her. In the same way that Jesus lovingly, thoughtfully, and joyfully served his bride, so a Christian man should pursue the woman he is interested in.

There are three things that to learn from the way Jesus pursued his bride.

Submission to God's Will

Nothing that Jesus did was outside of the will, desire, and plan of his Father. Better yet, Jesus fully submitted to the will that his Father had for his life and chose to follow God's plans for himself rather than his own. Jesus trusted God, was fully aligned to God's will, and constantly reminded himself of the mission God had given him.

In becoming the perfect sacrifice for humanity, Jesus knew that fully submitting to his Father's plan would bring the most glory to God. In the same way, you and I should try to live a life like Christ in which we completely surrender ourselves to our heavenly Father. Our jobs, ministries, and even our relationships with women are indeed not about us, but rather about bringing the greatest amount of glory to God.

Passionate Love

One of the things that we see during our Lord's life here on earth is how passionate he was for his bride. Jesus loved others, and he loved the church.

We see this manifested in many ways. Jesus loved his bride so much that he was willing to pray for her. Jesus set aside time to ask his Father's providence to be on his bride. Jesus also was willing to set aside his self-interest for the life of his church. He persevered through torture and injustice to show his love for his bride. In the same way, Christian men should display genuine interest in the woman they want to marry by finding ways to publicly and privately display love to her.

Ongoing Commitment

The beautiful thing about Jesus pursuing his bride is how Jesus continues to love his bride two thousand years later. Jesus was wedded to his bride, the church, during the first century AD. Now, as he is seated at the right hand of God, Christ is still available for those who love him.

Jesus intercedes on our behalf, pursues us when we are lost, and forgives us when we are wrong. These things are not just limited to a Christian one time in his life, but rather are available to a man every moment of his life. The relationship between the man and woman should be characterized by the continuous pursuit of the woman by the man. Men should be available for their wives, ready to listen, and eager to serve them in their needs. Men should be quick to forgive the offenses and wrongdoings of their brides and quick to confess their own.

I encourage you to seek to become like Christ and pursue him in all your endeavors. Don't just look to Christ for advice or help with pursuing a woman, rather orchestrate your entire life to look like Christ's. As you spend time with Christ, learning from and seeking to become like him, you should in turn begin to adopt the same principles and methods in pursuit of a bride like Jesus.

Remaining rooted in Christ is the anthem once again. Be a disciple of him. Learn from him, know more about him, be like him. Above all else in this world—including wealth, fame, status, health, or a woman—pursue Christ with everything you have. He will direct your paths and he will give you the desires of your heart as they are congruent with his own will (Prov. 16:3). Pursue Jesus because he is what matters most.

A Question
Are you willing to show sacrificial love to other men and women within the body of Christ?

A Single Shift
Don't assume a future relationship will just play out as it should. Make a plan. Ask God for help, and then write down some actions and activities that are consistent with a godly pursuit of a wife.

A Prayer
Jesus, thank you for your perfect example of pursuit. Thank you for pursuing me on my worst days and for initiating a relationship with me for eternity. Build a desire within me to learn more about how you pursue your bride. Amen.

Chapter 25

When to Pursue

For years, I have been the guy who said, "The grass is greener on the other side," until one day someone told me that the grass on the other side was turf and it wasn't all it was cracked up to be.

There's no doubt we treat our relationship life the same way. If you've been a part of the church for a while, you may feel like marriage is the crown jewel of life, since marriage is elevated so much in the church setting. Or, if you're living with single guys and your community is comprised of other singles, you might feel like being single is better than being married.

As you consider pursuing a woman, keep in mind that marriage and singleness alike seasons that God calls us to. They are equally important and equally valuable. In 1 Corinthians 7:7, Paul writes, "I wish that all of you were as I am. But each of you has your own gift from God; one has this gift, another has that" (NIV). Both marriage and singleness are gifts from God, and both are conducive to carrying out the purpose of God.

Some men are truly gifted to remain single for their entire lives. Paul says in 1 Corinthians that a single man is able to be devoted to the Lord's affairs since he is not concerned with trying to please his own wife (7:32-33). Yet Paul also encourages and promotes the union of a man and a woman in marriage (1 Cor. 7:1-5, Eph. 5:31). Marriage and singleness are both designed by God and have the potential to be used by God for his own glory. We should make an effort not to idolize one of these statuses over the others.

Your highest value doesn't come from a wife or from your closest friends. Your greatest accomplishment isn't to be married or to be successful or productive in singleness. Rather your highest value is to be pursuing a life of holiness for God. When you understand this, you might be ready to pursue a woman.

To Each His Own Season

It's important to also recognize that every person has their own seasons. If you're like me, you might have felt pressure to get married because all your friends or siblings were. As certain fruits are only available in particular seasons of the year, in God's economy, people each have their own season as well. Each person has a timeline for their life that is unique to him or her. The events that take place, the relationships that form, and the challenges that arise are unique to an individual and cannot and will not happen in the same timing to someone else. I think it's so interesting how many of us want our futures to be the same as our neighbors', yet we are glad that our pasts were different. But we must understand that it is because our pasts have been different that our future will look different too.

Throughout 1 Corinthians 7, Paul suggests multiple routes for the members of the church in Corinth to take. He commands men to remain single but shortly thereafter, he commands a man to marry a woman! Paul knows he is not talking to one person, but rather he is speaking to an entire church—a church filled with dozens of different stories and timelines.

Comparing yourself to others' life seasons is the easiest way for you to miss out on the season of life God has placed you in right now. There is a specific beginning and end to the seasons that will take place in your life, and they are much different than the schedule of your neighbor's seasons. Ecclesiastes 3:1 tells us, "There is a time for everything, and a season for every activity under the heavens" (NIV). Each person has their own unique seasons, and you must learn to be content with the seasons God brings to your life.

Changing Lanes Requires Correct Motive

If you've driven through a major city on a large highway before, you have probably seen the driver who restlessly switches lanes repeatedly. They move from your lane to the one to the left, then they switch back to your lane, leaving you shaking your head and wondering if the driver is actually effective in all his lane switching. When someone decides to move from one lane of life into the next—whether in a relationship, career, or otherwise—they must check their motivations before making that change.

Most of us like to assume we have the right motivations before we do something, but good actions with the wrong heart is dangerous. I have seen many men pursue a relationship for completely the wrong reasons. Some have wanted to get married so that they can merely relieve themselves sexually or have someone who can constantly give them the praise, attention, and affirmation they crave. Building a relationship on these motives is a recipe for ruin.

In 1 Corinthians 7, Paul suggests an array of actions to the people in Corinth. To some he suggests marriage; to some he suggests remaining single. But before he suggests any of these actions, he gives advice based on the motivations of the people.

So as one single man may go all-in, making the most of every opportunity in that time of his life, it isn't wrong for him to seek or even hope for a relationship. I have met countless men who are content in their single years, but at the same time, they are eager and excited about the possibility of marriage one day.

The key here is understanding and operating from your true identity. The reason many men want to switch from lane to lane or from one relationship status to the other is because they place too much weight and value on how their identity and worth would shift if they were in a relationship. If you are rooted in Christ, you can be outrageously content in your single years while at the same time anticipating marriage.

Go Where You Can Find the Most Holiness

What we see throughout 1 Corinthians 7 is Paul prescribing different solutions to different people in the church. Notice that every command is rooted in holiness. There are many different routes one can take in a relationship, and choosing the one that leads to you being the most holy is the route you should take.

Holiness is becoming more like Christ, becoming more sanctified, and becoming less conformed to the patterns of this world. As disciples of Christ, the goal should be to become more holy. Holiness is us running to the rich satisfactions and pleasures of Christ while simultaneously fleeing from the counterfeit satisfactions of the world. As Paul encourages the church in Corinth to do so, as you live in your single season, you must purify yourself of everything that contaminates the body and spirit (2 Cor. 7:1).

When you, as a single man, look at the different options you have for your relationship status, you should ask yourself which decision will lead to you becoming more holy. If pornography and sexual immorality fill your time, then it might be best to remain single as you work to weed out such actions. If you are growing in holiness, and you believe you can maintain a pursuit of holiness in the confines of marriage, then moving closer to that season could be your next step.

A Question
How have you grown significantly in holiness as a single man, and will you continue to pursue holiness in the context of dating a woman?

A Single Shift
Consider the women you have been interested in the past, as well as any you may be interested in now. How has your holiness and her holiness factored into your actions? Would a relationship with the person you are currently interested in lead you both nearer to God?

A Prayer
Lord, thank you for your Word and how clear it is to us today. Thank you for allowing me to be a disciple of Christ. I ask that you would help me to pursue holiness above all things and that you would check my motive and heart for wanting to pursue a woman. Help me to avoid comparing myself to others and empower me to make the wise decisions for myself that yield

growth in holiness. Amen.

Chapter 26

How and Where to Pursue

If you discover that you are not called to a life of singleness, then by default, you are called to a life of marriage. Thus, if you're called to marriage, you should not make it a point to remain single for the rest of your life. This would be unhealthy and disobedient as it relates to God's call for your life.

However, every man will be single at some point in his life. Many people will be single for the majority of their lives. Once you have chosen to honor the season of singleness and to make the most of every opportunity, it is likely that the opportunity to pursue a great woman will emerge.

I have heard countless stories from people all over the country who tell me they met their spouse during a season when they weren't looking for a spouse. Instead, these people were living a single life where they dove deeper into their relationship with the Lord and where they made the most of every opportunity. Many of these people began to think that they might remain single for a lifetime and even began to be concerned that they were "too content" being single.

This is probable in your life too. I am willing to bet that if you truly go head deep into your single season and you find yourself so content that you forget to look for a woman out there, that is when you will find the woman whom you want to pursue.

I hope that this is how it happens for you. I hope that in reading this book, you are inspired and equipped to make the most of the season that God has you right now, and while doing so, if you're called to marriage, a great woman is introduced to you.

So, what do you do when you meet this great woman? Well, hopefully you will be so content and joy-filled in living your single life that, at first, you might immediately write her off. But like I said, if you know you are not called to a life of singleness and are indeed called to a life of marriage, then it is noble of you to take a courageous step of faith and try pursuing her.

The pursuit of a woman works best when you're pursuing Christ first and foremost. From that foundation you are able to show her the same amount of love, sacrifice, and commitment that Christ has shown to you.

Now, it's okay if a woman pursues you initially, but don't let this become a norm in your relationship with her. I know many women who have taken the first move with a man who is completely oblivious, yet later they were able to submit to his leadership.

If you find yourself interested in a girl, don't wait until you know if she likes you or not. Begin the pursuit. Show her you are interested by asking her out to a meal or maybe by buying her flowers or a coffee. For many Christian guys, things can move fast, so as you initiate your pursuit, here are some things to keep in mind.

Crystal Clear Isn't Clear Enough

Women deserve clarity, and to be unclear is to be unkind. Let's be honest, guys do too. But men are the ones who are to lead by creating a culture of clarity in a relationship. The clearer you can be about your intentions, the faster you can move through the dating cycle. In today's world, it's very easy for men to sit back and let the women call the shots, but a lack of male leadership in the early stages of a relationship encourages all sorts of future issues in marriage. As the leader of the pursuit, you have the opportunity to establish clear communication.

When you begin pursuing a woman, let her know your intentions. You are not starting to talk to her to gain attention or have a new best friend; you're beginning this relationship with a purpose in mind.

Making it clear involves communicating your intentions to date, but it also means defining dating and what that means for each of you. The way you view dating might differ from her view of dating. Make it a point to consistently be clear about the status of your relationship, your feelings, and your intentions. If you feel like you are constantly stating the obvious, then you're doing it right.

Persistent but Not Bothersome

Do you remember how Jesus pursued you? There were probably a handful of times where Jesus tried to engage in a more meaningful relationship with you, but you might have ignored the call. But this didn't stop him. Within the context of dating, if you're really interested, pursue like Jesus and do not stop. Show your love through your actions of pursuing.

You don't want to overdo it and pursue so much that she feels like she is being hunted. Instead, make a point to understand what kind of attention she wants, and do those things for her. Some of the ways that you are not immediately inclined to pursue her might be some of the very acts that bring her the most joy. Become a student of her and ask her questions. Learn what she likes and doesn't like and show genuine interest in her. If it's quality time, then spend time together. If it's flowers, then send flowers. Every woman will be different, but every woman will appreciate pursuit. If she asks you questions, give her thoughtful answers and let her learn about you at the same time. Doing this will help you push through the dating process quicker.

If she becomes uninterested, then you'll know either by her words or her actions. If you've built a culture of clear communication, you'll know. If that's the case, don't become creepy or weird by bothering her or trying to force something on her. Respect where she is in life and understand that God is still by your side and is working in ways that you don't see. Don't let Satan trick you into thinking that there is something wrong with you personally. Remember your identity and know that she has a relationship with the Lord too. God might be doing something in her life, and you don't want to take that away from her. Ask God to show you if and when you should stop pursuing a woman if the season or timing or relationship isn't quite right.

When Is Marriage the Goal?

If you find yourself romantically interested in someone and the two of you have expressed a shared desire to be in a relationship, then marriage should be the goal. As a man, you should strive to graciously and lovingly lead the relationship toward the target of marriage.

If you are single and feel called to a life of singleness, then marriage should never be a goal for you. If you are single and do not feel called to a life of singleness, then marriage should be a goal and something you strive toward. But your ultimate goal in either case should be pursuing holiness and submitting to God's will.

Indeed, it should be the chief goal of all men to fear God and obey his commandments. Jesus tells us that marriage is not eternal, but our love for one another and for God is (Matt. 22:30). You and I will face God one day and give an account for how we maximized and invested in the seasons that God has placed us in.

Are you ready to fully go all-in on this season of life? Can you invest the bags of gold that you have been entrusted with and create a return on the investment that you make right now? The great news is that God is gracious enough to always give us another chance, and he is willing to give us the tools we need to live a life that honors him. You can do this, and you can find unbelievable contentment in your singleness right now. Let us build a life that pursues what truly matters the most!

A Question
What would it look like for you to live a life so content with being single that you forget about dating and looking for a woman?

A Single Shift
Ask a trustworthy woman (a married women would be best) about how to lead a relationship with clarity. Ask her about how to be clear and what you should be clear about with a woman you are interested in.

A Prayer

Lord, thank you for placing me on earth for such a time as this. Help me to submit to your will rather than my own and to build a life that is truly focused on your kingdom. As I pursue a woman, a daughter of God, help me to be intentional, gentle, caring, and compassionate toward her. Help me to continue to pursue you as I consider pursuing another woman. Amen.

Notes

Chapter 4
1 Strauss, Mark L. 2007. Four Portraits, One Jesus. Grand Rapids, Michigan: Zondervan, 151.
2 Ibid, 130.
3 See Deuteronomy 22:5
4 Pearcey, Nancy R, The Toxic War on Masculinity: How Christianity Reconciles the Sexes (Grand Rapids:Baker Books, 2023), 15.

Chapter 8
5 Linder, Jannik. "Pornography Industry Statistics." GITNUX. June 29, 2024. https://gitnux.org/pornography-industry-statistics/.
6 Ibid.
7 Black, Sam. "The Porn Circuit." Covenant Eyes, (2020). Accessed June 29, 2024.

Chapter 9
8 Black, Sam. "The Porn Circuit." Covenant Eyes, (2020). Accessed June 29, 2024.

Chapter 10
9 See Matthew 21 when Jesus clears the temple.
10 Delony, John. 2020. Redefining Anxiety: What It Is, What It Isn't, and How to Get Your Life Back. Ramsey Press.
11 Finkelhor, D., Hotaling, G., Lewis, I. A., & Smith, C. (1990). Sexual abuse in a national survey of adult men and women: Prevalence, characteristics and risk factors. Child Abuse & Neglect 14, 19-28. doi:10.1016/0145-2134(90)90077-7

Chapter 12
12 Groeschel, Craig. "Can You Trust God?" Sermon at Life.Church, Edmond, OK, October 25, 2020.

Chapter 13
13 I recommend giving through Compassion International (www.compassion.com).

14 Check out Ephesians 12:17-20

Chapter 15

15 Quarterly Report on Household Debt and Credit." New York Fed. May 1, 2019. https://doi.org/https://www.newyorkfed.org/medialibrary/interactives/householdcredit/data/pdf/hhdc_2019q1.pdf.

16 "Millennials and Retirement." Ramsey Solutions. September 27, 2021 doi.org/https://www.ramseysolutions.com/retirement/millennials-research.

17 "Living Paycheck to Paycheck Is a Way of Life for Majority of U.S. Workers, According to New CareerBuilder Survey." CareerBuilder. August 24, 2017. https://doi.org/https://press.careerbuilder.com/2017-08-24-Living-Paycheck-to-Paycheck-is-a-Way-of-Life-for-Majority-of-U-S-Workers-According-to-New-CareerBuilder-Survey.

18 "The State of Personal Finance in America Q2 2023." Ramsey Solutions. November 26, 2023. https://doi.org/https://www.ramseysolutions.com/budgeting/state-of-personal-finance.

19 Ramsey, Dave. Baby Steps Millionaires. (Nashville: Ramsey Press, 2022).

20 I use the EveryDollar app.

21 Head on over to RamseySolutions.com to check out free articles, apps, and podcasts.

Chapter 16

22 "Exercise: 7 Benefits of Regular Physical Activity." Mayo Clinic. August 6, 2023. https://doi.org/https://www.mayoclinic.org/healthy-lifestyle/fitness/in-depth/exercise/art-20048389.

23 Whitney, Donald. 1991. Spiritual Disciplines for the Christian Life. NavPress.

24 Maxwell, John C. 2014. Good Leaders Ask Great Questions. Center Street.

25 The chocolate-chip peppermint milkshake from Chick-fil-A is the world's best milkshake. In my opinion.

Chapter 17

26 Cathy, Truett S. 1989. It's Easier to Succeed Than to Fail. Thomas Nelson, Inc.

Chapter 18
27 Fidell, Miles. "I Can't Do This Alone." Sermon at Auburn Community Church, Auburn, AL, May 17, 2020.
28 Ibid.

Chapter 19
29 Horner, Bob, Ron Ralston, and David Sunde. 1996. The Promise Keeper at Work. Focus on the Family Publishing.
30 Maxwell, John C. The 15 Invaluable Laws of Growth: Live Them and Reach Your Potential. (New York: Center Street, 2014).

Chapter 20
31 Piper, John. Let the Nations Be Glad! (Grand Rapids: Baker Academic, 2023).

Acknowledgements

This book would not have been possible without prayers and input from so many individuals. I'd like to thank a few of them here.

From early morning airports breakfasts, to late night texts, I would like to thank Kyle Dennard for the way you challenged and advised me with respect to all the details of this book.

Thank you to Jacob Fierer who helped me brainstorm book titles and clearly articulate the message I had for single guys.

Thank you for my dad and encouragement you have been and the honesty you have given me throughout the book writing process.

And now, as a married man, I would like to thank my wife, Milena, for believing in me and supporting and encouraging me to get this book out! Thanks for giving me time and space to work on this project and for your fervent prayers as we launched this together.

I thank God that he has allowed me the time, experience, and resources to produce this work and that he unconditionally loves me despite how imperfect my single years were. May he receive all the glory and praise!

ALSO BY
Sam McManus

Stop praying away your single years.

Discover 75 unique prayers for the single man and start changing your life today.

www.ingramcontent.com/pod-product-compliance
Lightning Source LLC
Chambersburg PA
CBHW060601080526
44585CB00013B/649